Historic

THEATERS

of the

TENNESSEE
TRI-CITIES

Historic
THEATERS
of the
TENNESSEE
TRI-CITIES

ROBERT SORRELL

THE
History
PRESS

Published by The History Press
Charleston, SC
www.historypress.com

First published 2025

Manufactured in the United States

ISBN 9781467158053

Library of Congress Control Number: 2024945303

Notice: The information in this book is true and complete to the best of our knowledge. It is offered without guarantee on the part of the author or The History Press. The author and The History Press disclaim all liability in connection with the use of this book.

For my family.

CONTENTS

INTRODUCTION

*T*heater in the Tri-Cities region of Northeast Tennessee and Southwest Virginia is a vast and varied subject. Its history includes everything from early minstrel shows and vaudeville performances during the antebellum period to the modern multiplex movie houses of the twenty-first century.

This book examines the region's historic theaters, including both stage and movie houses, as well as theatrical organizations. The history of the theater in the Tri-Cities closely relates to the region's overall history, from its early founding and Industrial Revolution growth of the nineteenth century to the twentieth century when movie houses served as focal points in growing downtown business districts. By the mid-twentieth century, local downtown districts had begun to lose business, and theaters followed, moving to the region's outskirts and suburbs.

The Tri-Cities region, which straddles the state line of Tennessee and Virginia, consists of Bristol, Johnson City and Kingsport, as well as the surrounding communities and counties. The region is Tennessee's fifth-largest metropolitan area and has a population of more than a half-million people, according to the U.S. Census Bureau.

A rural Native American population resided in the area when pioneers first settled in the region in the mid-1700s. At that time, pioneers from the original American colonies headed west, crossed the ridges and passes of the Appalachian Mountains and found new homes in what became the Tri-Cities region.

The pioneers brought not only their families to the area but also their cultures. Many of the pioneers were of Scottish-Irish ancestry and enjoyed poetry, music, comedy and drama.

By the 1800s, decades after the United States' independence, the region's towns and cities had begun to grow; railroads were constructed, and business and industry emerged. Local residents gathered at locations in the center of the area's towns to share stories, perform songs and entertain one another as well as rally, debate and pray.

The region's earliest theater venues, where residents gathered, were often primitive. In the late nineteenth and early twentieth centuries, theaters occupied a variety of buildings, including schools, gymnasiums, stores, office buildings and religious facilities. Some theaters were simply set up on vacant lots where performances were held under canopies and tents or directly in the sunlight or moonlight. Theatrical performances included minstrel shows, vaudeville acts, burlesque, comedy, drama, music and medicine shows, where a touring act featured entertainment and medical treatments.

Around the turn of the century, the region was home to a few opera houses, auditorium halls and smaller stage venues. The theaters, such as the Jobe Opera House in Johnson City and the Harmeling Opera House in Bristol, hosted all types of entertainment, as well as political rallies and church services.

The advent of moving pictures led to a new era of theater in the Tri-Cities region.

There is no one person who definitively invented the movie or the movie theater, but in 1891, Thomas Edison's company successfully demonstrated a prototype of the Kinetoscope. The new technology enabled one person at a time to view moving pictures. A few years later, in Paris, France, a couple inventors used a device to project moving pictures to a paying audience.

Film slowly was introduced to American audiences, including those in the Tri-Cities region, but once it caught on, people flocked to their local movie house for entertainment.

Movie theaters in the Tri-Cities often changed and varied and have included converted dramatic theaters and storefront venues, such as nickelodeons, grand downtown movie palaces, suburban single and twin cinemas and state-of-the-art multiscreen megaplexes.

Newspaper articles around the dawn of the twentieth century detail some of the first moving picture, or film, presentations in the Tri-Cities. A failed exhibition in Elizabethton and a Johnson City dentist's hand-projected film display were among some of the region's first introductions to film.

A trolley travels down Main Street in downtown Johnson City, Tennessee, during the early twentieth century. The Edisonia Theatre operated along the thoroughfare. *Tom Roberts*.

The early twentieth century brought nickelodeon theaters to the Tri-Cities. The nickelodeon, named after the five-cent cost to view a show, was considered the first type of indoor exhibition space dedicated to showing projected motion pictures. During the warmer months, residents also headed to the nearest temporary air dome tent to watch a movie or a vaudeville show that had stopped in town via the railroad.

As movies gained popularity and technology improved, theaters became more prominent in the region. Many of the movie theaters built after World War I and into the 1920s and 1930s were grand spectacles. They featured modern projection and sound equipment, comfortable seats, bright and glossy design, giant glistening chandeliers and art deco architecture.

A few of the grand movie palaces of the day remain open in the new millennium in the Tri-Cities, including the Paramount Theatre in Bristol, the Capitol Theatre of Greeneville and the Bonnie Kate Theatre of Elizabethton.

In addition to the era's movie houses, the region also saw the development of the Barter Theatre in the 1930s. The Abingdon-based venue, which has been named the official state theater of Virginia, has received countless accolades throughout its history and is the nation's longest-running professional theater.

It was during the mid-twentieth century that delicious-buttered movie popcorn became a hit and blockbuster movies started to become all the rave. The term *blockbuster* was first introduced to the American lexicon in the 1940s.

The Paramount Theatre is a grand movie house on State Street in downtown Bristol, Tennessee. Theatre Bristol is next to the Paramount. *Author photo*.

By the mid-1900s, as in other American cities, the region's downtown districts began to lose business, the streets became a bit seedy and urban decay began to set in. The once grand movie houses, like the Majestic Theatre of Johnson City and the Columbia Theatre of Bristol, shuttered and were eventually demolished due to dangerous conditions and urban-renewal plans.

Slow Actors Crossing: A sign on Main Street in Abingdon, Virginia, warns drivers about actors crossing the street to reach the Barter Theatre. *Barter Theatre*.

Residents also discovered the fun and privacy of the drive-in movie theater, which were prevalent through the mid- and late 1900s. Practically every community in the Tri-Cities once had at least one drive-in venue where families could lounge under the stars, sit in their cars and trucks, enjoy a few snacks and drinks and enjoy a movie or two.

The mid- to late 1900s saw the development of suburban movie theaters. Developers looked away from downtown districts and constructed larger single-screen and multiscreen venues, such as the Holiday Cinema in Bristol, the Parkway Cinema in Johnson City and Martin Theatre in Kingsport. In the 1970s, movie theaters also opened in the region's new malls, which took even more business away from downtown districts.

As the new century approached, the early suburban theaters began to close, including those in the region's malls. New multimillion-dollar state-of-the-art movie theaters opened in the Tri-Cities, such as the Pinnacle 12 Marquee Cinemas in Bristol and AMC Johnson City 14. The modern theaters have been successful despite an increase in streaming movie services and home entertainment.

The Bays Mountain Drive-In was one of several drive-in theaters operating during the twentieth century in the Tri-Cities region. *City of Kingsport Archives.*

The Pinnacle 12 Marquee Cinemas is a modern movie-plex in the Pinnacle shopping, dining and entertainment complex in Bristol, Tennessee. *From the* Bristol Herald Courier.

The new century also brought about the restoration of several regional stage and movie theaters, including the State Theatre of Kingsport and Jackson Theatre of Jonesborough.

Aside from indoor stage theaters and movie theaters, the region has had its share of outdoor dramas and an assortment of specialty theaters. In fact, the Tri-Cities is home to the official outdoor dramas of Tennessee and Virginia. A few unique theaters, such as the auditorium at the International Storytelling Center in Jonesborough and the rustic venue at the Carter Family Fold, add to the region's theatrical amenities.

While professional theater companies have entertained residents and the movies have wowed audiences, local community theaters have also long delighted the Tri-Cities. The region has been home to several community theaters and little theater groups, including Tennessee's oldest continuously producing theater company in Johnson City. Numerous groups remained active into the twenty-first century, including several revitalized organizations.

For some residents, the only dramatics theater they have ever been introduced to took place at a local college campus. Several colleges and universities in the Tri-Cities region have theater programs as well as large auditoriums. The region's theater history includes college theater programs from the nineteenth century to today.

The Kingsport Theatre Guild is one of several community theater organizations to operate in the Tri-Cities region. *City of Kingsport Archives.*

The theater in the Tri-Cities has had quite a journey, and its history has had its share of trivial and turbulent times, but it has had something for everyone.

1

EARLY THEATERS

The Harmeling Opera House in the 500 block of State Street in Bristol, along the Tennessee and Virginia state line, was widely regarded as one of the most successful theaters in the early history of the Appalachian Mountains region. By the time it opened in the late nineteenth century, downtown Bristol was flourishing, and several businesses were opening, according to the National Register of Historic Places nomination form for the Bristol Commercial Historic District.

The Harmeling attracted visitors from around the region, as well as those traveling via the railroad. It had the largest seating capacity in the region at the time with about one thousand seats. It was the "neatest and most conveniently arranged" opera house between Lynchburg, Virginia, and Chattanooga, Tennessee, according to an article in the *Chattanooga Daily Times*.

Charles Harmeling originally opened the venue, which had an auditorium on the second floor, according to former *Bristol Herald Courier* writer Robert Loving.

In January 1890, Tennessee governor Robert "Bob" L. Taylor gave the dedication speech at the opera house's grand opening, which also featured a performance by the Mendelssohn Quintette Club of Boston, Massachusetts. The group was one of the most active and widely known chamber ensembles in the country.

"This company of distinguished artists is too well known to need a description," the *Comet* newspaper of Johnson City reported.

State Street in Bristol has been home to numerous theaters over the years, including the Harmeling Opera House and Paramount Theatre. *Alex Garrison.*

The first affair at the Harmeling was "strictly white tie" and included many distinguished guests, according to later written histories published in the *Bristol Herald Courier*. In addition to the governor, two congressmen also attended the opening. The first program was printed on a piece of fine cloth. People came by train from faraway points, paying what was then an expensive five-dollar admission price.

Bud Phillips, a Bristol historian, said he obtained a ticket that notable Bristol merchant H.P. King purchased and used for the first night's program.

Karl Harmeling, nephew of the opera house's founder, recalled a memory of a fire at the theater, according to Loving.

"I was a member of the Eagle Volunteers, the Bristol Virginia fire department," Harmeling told Loving. "The fire started and destroyed a novelty store next door, then caught the roof and also damaged the stage of the opera house."

The opera house eventually closed as a playhouse during World War I, and bookings were then transferred to the new Columbia Theatre on nearby Fifth Street. An agreement was made in which no more plays would be shown at the venue, the *Bristol Herald Courier* said.

The site later experienced a succession of new occupants, including department stores, according to Bristol historian Tim Buchanan. The present building at the site was constructed in 1948, according to the nomination form.

Prior to the Harmeling's opening, community gatherings, such as plays and musical events, were held at two local auditoriums: the hall at the Reynolds tobacco factory and Conway Hall, which was located along Fifth Street, just south of the state line.

Conway Hall featured the city's first large stage and auditorium and could seat about three hundred people, Loving said. It provided a performance space for operas, concerts, traveling shows and home-grown performances. Eventually, Conway Hall burned to the ground, and the town's fire hall was erected at the site, Loving noted. The fire department also eventually relocated.

Tobacco manufacturer Major A.D. Reynolds, who employed hundreds of Bristolians, constructed a four-story building on Fourth Street, now known as Martin Luther King Jr. Boulevard, in the 1800s. On the top floor, he built an auditorium with seating for about three hundred people and a large stage. The building no longer stands.

After Thomas Edison's Vitascope projector began gaining traction around the beginning of the twentieth century, moving pictures were introduced to the public. At that point, theaters in the Tri-Cities region began to show Vitascope movie productions as well as vaudeville shows and other stage presentations.

After 1900, the nickelodeon theater, which got its name from five-cent shows, became a popular entertainment concept in the United States, including in the Tri-Cities region. About a decade later, those storefront theaters were replaced by larger movie houses.

The old Fairyland Theatre operated for several years along State Street, but its exact dates are difficult to determine. Newspaper records show the theater was at least in operation between 1905 and 1915. It was managed by C.H. Thomas.

The theater closed briefly in February 1907 when the motion picture machine was damaged, according to the *Bristol Herald Courier*.

"We have ordered Edison's best machine," the theater's management said. "Look for something good when it arrives."

The Fairyland reopened in March 1907, and the *Bristol Herald Courier* said the venue "which is well conducted in every aspect is winning much praise from its patrons."

The moving pictures and the pictures illustrating popular songs appeared lifelike, the newspaper said. The Fairyland showcased a variety of motion pictures, including films of auto races at Brighton Beach and the India Rubber Men, comedies and acrobats. The venue also featured vaudeville and musical acts.

In the summer of 1908, the newspaper reported the theater's motion pictures and illustrated songs were growing in popularity. The attendance at both afternoon and evening performances had been unusually good, and several times the house had been taxed to its capacity.

In 1915, the Central Amusement Company, which also owned the nearby Eagle and Olympic theaters, purchased the Fairyland.

That same year, the Fairyland was chosen to show a motion picture about how cement is used, according to the *Bristol Herald Courier*. City commissioners from the Holston Street Improvement District went to Knoxville, Tennessee, to inspect street work to determine the best path to improve the city's streets. The city obtained a film about cement and partnered with the Fairyland to show the film, which was "educational in nature" and was shown to "impress the businessmen and property owners" with the importance of making permanent streets.

The Gem, a nickelodeon, was another one of Bristol's earliest theaters. It was located along State Street at its intersection with Moore Street on the Virginia side of the state line. A newspaper article from 1907 said the Gem Picture Show would offer several "new and beautiful" moving picture during the week "of the very best kind."

"Nothing is more conductive to pleasure than good, instructive moving pictures," said the *Bristol Herald Courier*.

The newspaper article continued, saying moving pictures were a source of "every increasing delight to young and old and deserve rank among wonders of our present age."

To attract more patrons, the Gem, which was open for a short time, held a variety of events, including drawings for prizes.

State Street was also home to the Elite Theatre. A venue known as the "Elite" electric theater, first operating in the Harmeling building on State Street, was featured in the February 9, 1908 issue of the *Bristol Herald Courier*. The theater had been sold to L.S. Jones, the article stated.

The following week, the newspaper reported that the Elite had a strong offering of high-class vaudeville acts. In addition, the article said the theater's management had reached an agreement with the Chicago Film Company to get the latest moving pictures.

Throngs of visitors continued to visit the Elite in 1908. During the spring, the manager, Harry Knox, donated 15 percent of the proceeds from shows to the proposed King's Mountain Hospital, a new hospital that eventually opened in Bristol in 1925.

In 1908, the *Bristol Evening News* reported that John C. Meany, a local businessman, was opening a new theater. It would be called the Elite Theatre and was in the 600 block of State Street, a building that had been home to the Turner drugstore. Meany's theater featured vaudeville acts and a new piano, the newspaper said.

The theater temporarily closed in 1909, according to the *Bristol Herald Courier*: "Mr. Meany closed the Elite last spring for the summer with the intention of returning in the early fall to start it again and is now here for that purpose. He earned a reputation last winter for high-class vaudeville and motion picture shows and is again at the service of the Bristol show-going public."

The Elite appears to have closed by 1911.

Bristol's residents could also enjoy an evening of entertainment at the Salvation Army, which operated the Citadel, a venue located on Seventh Street on the Tennessee side of the state line.

Various moving pictures on biblical subjects were shown at the Salvation Army in 1909. It featured a series of movies through the winter months, according to the *Bristol Herald Courier*. The programs were especially attracted to the children and young people of Bristol.

Like other communities in the Tri-Cities, several outdoor tent theaters, known as air domes, operated in Bristol. In 1908, the *Bristol Herald Courier* reported that one air dome theater would provide the strongest and best vaudeville ever presented in Bristol. It was located on Moore Street in Bristol, Virginia.

A partial list of those who performed included Billy Brown, a minstrel man, comedian and monologue artist; Miss Gardner, a singing and dancing soubrette, or a female performer who portrayed a flirtatious character; Happy George Lavine, a man who was said to make people happy by singing songs and telling jokes; and Gardner and Lawson, a pair of comedy sketch artists who sang and danced.

On one occasion, the Airdome presented *A Life's Revenge* by a stock company, which is a troupe of actors who perform regularly in a particular theater, presenting a different play every night. *A Life's Revenge* was a four-act play featuring melodrama and critical situations.

"It is thought by many who saw it last night to be the best play put on at the Airdome this season," the *Bristol Herald Courier* reported.

The largest crowd to ever attend a show at the Airdome was reported in September 1908. About 1,600 people went to the venue for a Ku Klux Klan event and a fiddlers contest. The *Bristol Herald Courier* said it was standing room only.

The Airdome presented its last show of 1908 in October. Under the management of James A. Cross, the proprietor, assisted by James D. Kilgore, the seasonal venue featured *The Devil*, a short film.

The pair reopened the "warm-weather playhouse" one year later at a site opposite the Hotel Burson, the newspaper said. The new air dome had a capacity of two thousand and would be semicircular in shape with an entry on Moore Street, the newspaper added.

Meany, who operated other venues in Bristol, managed the Airdome during the summer of 1910.

A separate air dome theater opened in 1909 on Seventh and Shelby Streets, adjoining the Salvation Army. It was operated by Earl B. Smith and Frank Lynn, according to the *Bristol Herald Courier*.

By 1914, another tent theater known as the Majestic Airdome had opened on Cumberland Street near the post office. It showcased "nothing but the best censored pictures," and special attention was given to ladies and children, the newspaper said.

Early Johnson City History

While Bristol served as a center of entertainment, the nearby city of Johnson City also provided quality entertainment for its citizens, as well as those who stopped in town via the railroad.

Johnson City was home to its own opera house around the turn of the twentieth century. At that time, like Bristol, Johnson City saw substantial growth due to the railroad, and it became home to a new National Soldiers Home.

Around 1884, about the same time Johnson City was incorporated by the State of Tennessee, Issac "Ike" T. Jobe opened an opera house at the corner of Main and Spring Streets in the center of the town. It was located a short distance from the railroad depot.

The opera house was on the second floor above the Gump Brothers clothing store, according to local historian Bob Cox. To enter the venue, Cox said guests had to enter through the store on the Main Street side of the building and climb the stairs to the auditorium. The lecture hall's use also included sporting activities and even once served as a courtroom, Cox said.

A sign on Main Street details the history of downtown Johnson City, including its theaters. The Wallace Theatre can be seen in the background. *Author photo*.

Jobe, who served as the mayor of Johnson City from 1882 to 1892, and the Gumps expanded the venue, eventually reaching nine hundred seats.

In 1885, the *Comet* newspaper reported that Jobe had purchased a "magnificent set of scenery" containing about thirty-six pieces for the opera house from a Chicago firm.

"With this scenery Jobe's Hall will be one of the nicest and best equipped in Tennessee," the *Comet* said.

In 1891, former Tennessee governor Robert "Bob" Taylor brought his lecture tour to the opera house, according to the *Comet*.

"The occasion had been looked forward to with great interest, and none were disappointed," the newspaper reported. "At the hour for the opening, the opera house was crowded to its utmost capacity with the representative intelligence and culture of the city and surrounding county."

By 1892, Harry Gump and John Mathes were managing the opera house, had made "needed changes" and were working to secure the best troupes possible, the newspaper said.

It is not clear whether Jobe's personal life affected the venue, but he was arrested and served time in jail beginning in 1899. He was convicted on charges related to using penalty envelopes, or the act of using government mail for private purposes. Prior to his arrest, Jobe had a fake obituary published in a Kentucky newspaper, the *Comet* reported. Jobe later died in 1919 in North Carolina.

During its heyday, the opera house scheduled traveling plays, community plays, opera and lectures, according to Ray Stahl, who wrote the book *Greater Johnson City: A Pictorial History*. It also served as a site for high school graduation ceremonies. Students would march from the high school to the opera house in white frocks and black suits to receive their diplomas, Stahl wrote.

In its later years, the opera house's popularity waned, which led the *Comet* to criticize the venue.

"The present opera house is not sufficient to meet the demands," the newspaper said. "It is true that we get a few fair companies, but one time does them. They cannot show off to advantage. The stage is so limited that it makes everything unsatisfactory."

The Gump brothers appear to have given up on the opera house by 1905, and the newspaper later reported that the Jobe heirs would remodel the frame building. The opera house space was converted into offices.

The building was eventually demolished, and new buildings have since been constructed at the site at the corner of Main and Spring Streets.

At the turn of the twentieth century, one motion picture house, the Minnehaha, operated in Johnson City. Dr. J.A. Denton, who later became a city commissioner, owned the theater. Although the silent pictures were short and sometimes offered two or three subjects on one reel, they became almost talkies, since at times Denton explained the pictures as they were being shown, according to an article in the *Johnson City Chronicle* on early theaters.

The early twentieth century also brought outdoor theater venues to Johnson City. The Electric Park Theatre entertained patrons in 1908 near downtown. The *Comet* reported that Johnson City could boast of a "real genuine" city attraction in the new theater, which had just opened on the corner of North Main Street and Fourth Avenue in the growing Carnegie section of the city.

Everything at the Electric Park Theatre was neat and clean, including the performances, and hundreds of electric lights turned night into day, the newspaper said. A large tent was erected at the site for performances, which drew huge crowds, and it featured comfortable seats. There were two performances a day, and cars ran every fifteen minutes from the National Soldiers Home to the theater until the last performance concluded.

In 1909, an air dome theater opened during the summer months in Johnson City along Roan Street between Main Street and the railroad tracks, according to newspaper articles. Similar to those in Bristol, the

Airdome venue was housed in a large tent. It featured heavy canvas tops and sides, which provided a cool and comfortable place to enjoy the program. The Airdome, which featured lives stage shows rather than moving pictures, was rainproof.

The Edisonia, which is often considered Johnson City's first premier movie house, opened in the 200 block of Main Street in downtown Johnson City in 1909. Today, the site is across the street from Majestic Park, which was once home to the Majestic Theatre. First operated by H.A. Colvin, the Edisonia featured vaudeville performances, such as comedy acts and jugglers, and plays before being converted into a silent movie house, the *Johnson City Press* said.

By 1912, businessman George W. Keys had bought the Edisonia from Colvin and remodeled it into what at that time was a modern theater. Silent pictures were run, and many of the features were two reels in length, the newspaper said.

In the 1920s, the theater changed its name to the Criterion because the owners got a "good deal on a huge sign" from the Criterion theater in Atlanta, Georgia, the newspaper said in 2015.

An advertisement in the May 2, 1926 issue of the *Johnson City Chronicle* acknowledged the Criterion's grand opening.

"The Criterion opens up its doors proudly, for without exaggeration or boasting it is one of the prettiest little theaters in the state," the advertisement

The Edisonia Theatre was one of Johnson City's earliest vaudeville and movie houses. It operated for decades on Main Street. *Tom Roberts.*

The Majestic Theatre and the Criterion Theatre faced each other along Main Street in downtown Johnson City. *Tom Roberts.*

states. "Everything is new, spotlessly clean. A visit will convince you of this, and it will be kept this way at all times. The policy will be good pictures, for the least money, and a price of five cents for children and ten cents for adults will be maintained."

Improvements included a metal ceiling, interior decorating, changes to the lobby and box office and new walls, a new screen setting, new motion picture projectors, new seats and recarpeting.

Hal Youngblood managed the reopening and said the theater would operate on a high-class basis with uniformed attendants, cleanliness, good pictures, polite service and a price that had made the old theater famous.

Following showings of *Fighting Texas* and *Devil Horse*, the Criterion closed in 1934 for a complete rebuild, but the theater never reopened.

The Dixie and Odeon Theatres operated near Fountain Square in downtown Johnson City at the beginning of the twentieth century. The theaters were housed in the same building, which was on the west side of the railroad tracks, close to where the Johnson City Farmers Market is now located and opposite the fountain. Several shops, restaurants and the former Arlington and Windsor hotels were located nearby.

"The Dixie Theatre, which has reopened under new management, has been pleasing crowds this week with a bill composed of high-class vaudeville, moving pictures, and illustrated songs," the *Comet* reported on January 27, 1910. "It's worth the money."

Later in 1910, the Dixie was managed by a couple local businessmen: Colvin, who also operated the Edisonia, and C.A. Goebel, who managed several popular theaters in the Tri-Cities.

"The Dixie is perhaps the swellest theater between Knoxville and Roanoke, having all the modern conveniences necessary to make it comfortable in every respect," the *Comet* said. Colvin announced he would secure some of the "best pictures and illustrated songs that money" could buy for his patrons.

When Goebel began managing the Dixie, he told the newspaper that he would present only strong, clean and attractive features, including "high class acts by people of known ability."

The Dixie often had two shows a day, including one at 2:00 p.m. and another usually around 6:30 p.m.

The Dixie Theatre appears to have been featured on a Sanborn Fire Insurance map for Johnson City that was published in 1913. A rectangular building is labeled "moving pictures" and was located near the railroad tracks. Sanborn maps were detailed maps of cities and towns across the country and were created to allow fire insurance companies to assess their total liability in an urbanized area. Today, they are a valuable research tool. Many of the theaters in the Tri-Cities during the first half of the twentieth century are featured on Sanborn maps.

In 1915, the venue reopened as the Odeon Theatre. The owner, Alex Wall, was described in the *Comet* as a "well-known moving picture man." The venue was thoroughly remodeled and featured a "comfortable and cozy" auditorium.

The Odeon opened with the movie *The Lure of the Mask*, and the newspaper said, "If Mr. Wall keeps up this class of pictures, he will no doubt play to crowded houses every day." The silent film, which was released in 1915, featured Harold Lockwood, Elsie Jane Wilson and Irving Cummings.

In early 1916, the Odeon brought in a new orchestra to provide sound to the silent films and other attractions.

"Those who visit the Odeon will get value received for their money," the *Comet* said. "First-class pictures and perfect order will be found at the Odeon at all times."

Wall closed the Odeon Theatre in May 1916, according to the *Comet*.

MEMORIAL HALL

First established in 1901 and opened in 1904, the Mountain Branch of the National Home for Disabled Volunteer Soldiers features one of the region's oldest and longest-serving theaters.

The campus is home to dozens of buildings, many of which have been renovated for modern uses, but some, like the Memorial Hall Theater, retain a number of original interior elements.

Also known as the Opera House, the structure was built in 1904 and has not only withstood the test of time but has also etched its name into the annals of architectural and cultural history, according to the U.S. Department of Veterans Affairs.

Designed by the renowned architect Joseph Freedlander in the Beaux-Arts style, the Memorial Hall Theater is a south-facing venue and is located just east of the chapel.

The *Comet* newspaper of Johnson City first reported on the theater in 1904. The auditorium could seat 1,200 people and cost about $60,000.

"The building is really an opera house and will be a very handsome one," the *Comet* reported.

Memorial Hall, a historic theater, is located on the U.S. Veterans Affairs campus in Johnson City. It was built in 1904. *Library of Congress.*

Memorial Hall in Johnson City features a luxurious auditorium with a large stage and proscenium, as well as big, comfortable chairs. *Library of Congress.*

The Memorial Hall Theater has remained a hub for community events for more than a century. Throughout the early 1900s, the theater hosted numerous dance recitals and theater productions that captivated audiences and left lasting memories, the Department of Veterans Affairs stated.

In the early 1900s, vaudeville acts, which featured live theater and comedy, often visited the theater. The acts arrived in Johnson City by train and offered free performances for the veterans at Mountain Branch.

There was no sound system at Memorial Hall during the early days. A live band provided the musical accompaniment, according to the Department of Veterans Affairs.

Walter P. Brownlow, the U.S. congressmen who was responsible for the Mountain Branch's development, played a pivotal role in securing musical companies to donate instruments and forming a band composed of veterans. The band performed every Wednesday evening and Sunday afternoon.

Many patrons traveled to Memorial Hall by trolley, which they could catch throughout Johnson City. They could enjoy the afternoon on the campus and dance and sing along to the band or watch a show.

The theater underwent renovations in the 1980s, which included replacing seats and carpets.

For several decades, Memorial Hall was leased by the Friends of Theatre at East Tennessee State University's Theater Department, making it a vital part of the local arts and culture scene. Many university-led plays were held at the theater. However, in 2018, a new chapter began when the VA's Maintenance Unit B moved into the theater, the Department of Veterans Affairs stated.

In 2020, the building received some upgrades, including the installation of new heating, ventilation and air-conditioning systems.

The theater remains intact. Its intricate curtains, elegant arches, French doors, curved stairways, stage, orchestra pit and ornate balconies continue to transport visitors to a bygone era of grandeur and sophistication, according to the National Register of Historic Places nomination form.

2

BRISTOL THEATERS

The movie industry experienced significant growth in the twentieth century, and people around the country went to theaters in droves. During that time, numerous movie houses opened throughout the Tri-Cities area, although many have since closed.

The old Columbia Theatre in downtown Bristol, Tennessee, was one of the finest movie houses in the region. All that remains today is a parking lot and memories. The theater, which was designed by prominent Bristol architect Thomas S. Brown, opened to the public on May 27, 1912.

It first featured vaudeville shows and photoplays but later introduced silent and sound films.

The theater was the dream of Robert L. Blevins, according to historian Bud Phillips, who wrote for the *Bristol Herald Courier*. As a youth, Blevins attended a program at the former Conway Hall, one of Bristol's earlier venues, and dreamed that he would one day build his own venue where more interesting shows would be performed, Phillips said.

His dream of creating an entertainment hall was realized in 1912, when he opened the Columbia Theatre on Fifth Street, near its intersection with State Street. Conway Hall was nearby.

The Columbia featured a large stage and box seats that were built on each side of the main floor, according to newspaper articles. Large glittering frescoes of angels surrounded by cherubs were painted on the theater's ceiling. It also featured the latest in lighting and outside displays.

The Columbia Theatre was a large vaudeville and movie theater in downtown Bristol, Tennessee, on Fifth Street. *George Stone.*

Phillips recalled seeing the colorful tiles that had been worked into the recessed front entry. The building was large and well decorated, Phillips wrote.

An advertisement in the city newspaper announced the Columbia's first show: "Opening of the Columbia Theatre, Monday May 27, Charles E. Mack, blackface comedian; Morse and Clark, lively piano-singing act; May Archer and Billy Car, some songs and photo plays."

The matinee cost ten cents, box seats were fourteen cents and children's seats were five cents, according to a newspaper advertisement. During the evening, general admission was ten cents, orchestra seats were twenty cents and box seats were thirty cents, the advertisement stated.

Another *Bristol Herald Courier* article shared the story of Arch Eades, a projectionist who worked at the Columbia when it first opened. There were no projectionists in Bristol when the Columbia first opened.

"We had only one projection machine and cranked it by hand, one reel at a time," Eades told the newspaper. "Between reels we would put on a slide reading, one minute to change reels."

Eades said it would take several minutes for the second reel to begin showing on the screen. Moviegoers were used to bad breaks, and occasionally, they would stomp their feet or whistle their impatience.

When storms swept through Bristol, moviegoers often sat in the dark until the lights came back on, he said.

Some of the best vaudeville acts were brought to Bristol, as it served as a stop between Roanoke, Virginia, and Knoxville, Tennessee. After vaudeville left Bristol, small musical shows known as tabs, which carried about twenty people, would come to the Columbia for two to three weeks, changing their acts every few days. Popular at the time, the tabs featured a variety of short musical comedies.

Eades also remembered when the famous minstrel shows and productions visited the Columbia. He recalled seeing *The Old Homestead* and *Polly of the Circus*. In addition, the Columbia booked some road shows, such as the Broadway production of Sigmund Romberg's *The Desert Song*.

In 1923, the Columbia held a new grand opening with manager Lee G. Garner of Washington, D.C. In addition, a new Hope-Jones organ was installed, as well as opera chairs and projection machines.

Phillips said the Columbia also began to put together a local quartet to go along with the shows, particularly silent movies. In addition, the projectionist would also fire a real pistol into a thick wooden block to go along with gunfight scenes, Phillips added.

A large parking lot can be found where the Columbia Theatre once operated in Bristol. The Birthplace of Country Music Association offices are located nearby. *Author photo*.

By 1925, C.A. Goebel had purchased the Columbia from J. Gutman, according to the *Bristol Herald Courier*. Goebel also owned the Isis, Cameo and Eagle theaters in Bristol.

Finally, in late 1957, when the lease expired, W.A. Wilson Jr., who had owned the theater for about six years, decided not to renew the contract. He closed the Columbia, the property was offered for sale and crews began removing seats and equipment, the newspaper reported.

The Columbia was later demolished and now serves as a parking lot near the administrative offices of the Birthplace of Country Music.

STATE STREET MOVIE HOUSES

Beginning in 1915, Fred Perryman and Goebel's Olympic Theatre operated for just a couple years along State Street in Bristol. The pair previously operated the Fairyland, according to the *Bristol Herald Courier*. The Olympic venue featured a glass screen, which was unusual for a theater.

The Olympic opened on March 18, 1915, with Marion Leonard in the six-reeler film *The Light Unseen*, as well as an orchestra performance.

Later, in July 1916, fire damaged the Olympic during a movie. Shortly before 10:00 a.m., several people yelled "Fire" as the theater began to fill with smoke. The house was full, and no one panicked, "although a few women began to cry," the *Bristol Herald Courier* said. The patrons rose from their seats and marched out of the theater in an orderly manner. Many waited along State Street as firefighters arrived.

Smoke billowed into the theater after a carbon broke in the movie projector as the operator was preparing to insert a new one. The broken carbon then fell against the reel of film being unwound and set it afire, the newspaper reported. The blaze spread to the insulated walls of the projection room but no further. Firefighters extinguished the blaze quickly, but the machine was destroyed. As a result, the theater reopened a few days later. The Olympic eventually closed in 1917.

The Eagle, Isis, State and Shelby theaters, which operated at various times in the twentieth century, were all located in the 500 block of State Street on the Virginia side of the state line.

The Eagle, which appears to have opened in 1910 and provided space for church services, was located in a three-story brick building that was constructed in 1890, according to newspaper articles.

According to CinemaTreasures.org, a website that showcases the world's historic theaters, the Eagle was featured in the 1926 edition of the *Film Daily Yearbook* and had 275 seats. The Eagle, which became a popular western and serial picture house, closed in 1927. It then became a billiard parlor, the website states.

In 1930, the Salvation Army began to host services in the former theater building because its auditorium on Fourth Street was not large enough for the increasing number of people in attendance. One year later, Goebel, who owned the Eagle and adjacent former Isis Theatre, said the two buildings would be remodeled into modern store buildings.

The Isis Theatre, which was next door to the Eagle and operated by C.A. Goebel, opened to the public on the afternoon of January 7, 1917. "The new Isis Theatre on State Street was given a most cordial welcome by the picture fans of this city," the *Bristol Herald Courier* said.

Uniformed ushers were stationed in the aisles of the new venue, which had been completed by construction crews one week earlier. A maid was also in attendance at the ladies' restroom, and music was furnished by a pipe organ, the newspaper said.

In 1923, the Isis installed a new Robert-Morton Organ, which was described as "one of the most wonderful instruments in the musical world."

The newspaper said movie fans and music lovers of Bristol had heard organs before, but they never heard one like the new one at the Isis, unless they had visited the larger theaters of America's biggest cities.

The *Film Daily Yearbook* listed the Isis Theatre in 1929, according to the CinemaTreasures.org website. It was not listed in the 1926 edition, the website states.

After the Isis closed in 1931, the site became the St. Regis restaurant, according to the *Bristol Herald Courier*. The building was completely remodeled and would provide space for dinner, dancing, bridge luncheons, club luncheons and banquets. It later then became the Sprinkles Café, which added a new fountain.

A few years later, on February 17, 1938, the State Theatre opened on State Street. In order to be the first person to purchase a ticket at the new theater, seventeen-year-old Johnnie Nelson stood for nine hours in front of the venue, according to the *Bristol Herald Courier*.

"I just wanted to be ahead of everybody else for at least once in my life," Nelson said.

The theater, which opened with *Mountain Music* starring Bob Burns and Martha Raye, featured both first-run productions and the return of second-run pictures. While not the largest in Bristol—it had a seating capacity of 397—the State was one of the city's most modern venues. The Publix-Bamford Corporation, which also managed the nearby Paramount, operated the State, the newspaper reported.

The State Theatre, as well as the nearby Shelby Theatre, were broken into and ransacked in 1955, according to a news report. Various items were stolen from both venues.

Owners appear to have closed the State Theatre in the mid-1950s. Handcraft One-House Cleaners was operating at the State's address by 1957, and it had become a bicycle repair shop by 1975. The current building features a circa 1970 storefront with large glass doors and display windows. The building's theater seats have been removed.

The Shelby Theatre operated during the mid-twentieth century, according to advertisements. By 1960, the movie house opened under new management. The *Bristol Herald Courier* reported that two businessmen, Don W. Owens of radio station WOPI and Bill Hagy of Nationwide Insurance, announced that they had purchased the theater from John W. Rogers. The pair said the building would keep the Shelby Theatre name as well as the policy of showing double features for each program.

Owens and Hagy, who created the Howe Theatre Corporation, then renovated the theater, including adding new seats. The Shelby was listed for sale by 1961. A newspaper advertisement said the owner was "leaving town" and would sacrifice the building for $4,000.

THE CAMEO

Farther down State Street, near Piedmont Avenue on the Virginia side of the line, the Cameo Theatre originally opened on March 30, 1975. The Cameo, an art deco–style venue, was originally designed with Colonial Revival influences and continued to be a working theater in the twenty-first century, according to the National Register of Historic Places.

Construction of the Cameo cost $125,000, according to an article announcing its opening. Its owner, C.A. Goebel, planned to devote the theater to motion pictures, vaudeville and "legitimate attractions." It became a popular vaudeville stop due to its easy access to the railroad, which passed through Bristol.

The grand sign and front façade of the Cameo Theatre can be seen in this vintage postcard of State Street in Bristol. *George Stone.*

The Cameo opened with *The Famous Marcus Show*, a program described as "the best musical venue in the whole wide world, the greatest collection of femininity ever assembled." Management also showed the silent movie *Secrets of the Night*, a 1924 silent film described as a murder mystery–melodrama comedy.

Edwin Albert Booth, who also managed the historic Bijou Theatre in Knoxville and others in Greeneville, served as the Cameo's manager.

Goebel's goal was to provide cozy, comfortable and home-like entertainment, and the theater ultimately had a capacity of seven hundred. He set out to equip the theater with "all of the conveniences" of large city theaters with more seating. To realize his goals, Goebel hired C.K. Howell of Richmond, Virginia, to design the Cameo. Howell had drawn plans for nearly one hundred theaters and was considered the most efficient theater architect in the South, according to the *Evening Herald Courier*.

The grand Cameo featured a main auditorium with four hundred seats, as well as a three-hundred-seat balcony. The seats were "just as desirable from every standpoint as those in the main auditorium."

Goebel said the theater's seating arrangement would allow him to set aside a section for "the high-class colored patronage." About 150 seats were arranged in the balcony for "colored people," Goebel said.

"These are just as good seats and as well located as those reserved for the white patronage," the *Bristol Herald Courier* reported. "In addition, the colored patrons were provided comfort conveniences and restrooms."

Goebel did not spare expense when installing seats. The chairs featured leather upholstery, box cushions and fifty-six springs in each seat. They were described as handsome and comfortable opera chairs.

The Cameo's mezzanine floor was described as an attractive feature in 1925. Divans, upholstered chairs, floor lamps and other furnishings adorned the section, which was just as attractive as any fine Bristol home, the newspaper said. The mezzanine's floor was covered in carpet, and canary birds, palm trees and cut flowers filled the room.

During opening week, the Cameo's manager arranged several movies for showings, including *Thief of Bagdad*, *Charlie's Aunt*, *Friendly Enemies*, *Three Women*, *The Sea Hawk* and *Oh Doctor*.

FLIGHT OF THE FILM

Early on, local theaters, including the Cameo, received films from distributors by automobile and train. Films from Charlotte, North Carolina, came to Bristol by train via Asheville, North Carolina, and Morristown, Tennessee, the *Bristol Herald Courier* reported.

In April 1938, the Cameo was planning to showcase the film *The Adventures of Tom Sawyer*, but the product did not arrive in time for afternoon showings. After failing to receive the film in time for showings, the Cameo's management and United Artists orchestrated delivery by air.

A plane crew from College Park, Maryland, flew the film to the Inter-City Airport in Bristol just ten minutes before a 7:20 p.m. showing. The Cameo's manager notified the airport of the plane's arrival, and Kelly Owen, the airport's manager, had everything ready to receive the plane and the film.

"We have had several unusual experiences in our 23 years in the theater business in Bristol, but this is the first time a film has ever been sent to us by airplane," James M. Goebel, the Cameo's manager, told the newspaper. It was the first time a theater in the Tri-Cities was known to receive a new film by airplane.

The Cameo stayed open for decades, but by 1982, the theater's popularity had waned. The owners said the theater would close due to poor economic factors and the increased difficulty to obtain quality movies.

"It's regrettable that this fine theater must close," co-owner Thomas Curtin Jr. told the *Bristol Herald Courier*. "The increased expense of operation has for some time been mounting to the point that it is much higher than the income, therefore it is just not profitable to continue to operate the Cameo."

Leading up to the closure, the theater showcased Walt Disney Company and other family entertainment films. The theater had long outlasted other movie houses in downtown Bristol as multiscreen operations opened.

The Cameo's age was a problem by the time it closed. Film distributors became reluctant to sell their new films to an old downtown theater.

In 1983, Glenn Pridemore rented the building and reopened the old theater with a showing of the cult classic *Night of the Living Dead*. Pridemore served as a mortician at the Akard Funeral Home in Bristol.

The theater closed a short time later, but John Stone reopened the Cameo in 1984, according to the *Bristol Herald Courier*. Stone, who also co-founded Mountain Empire Comics, operated the theater through 1985.

"The owner of the Cameo Theatre didn't expect to show blockbuster films or draw huge crowds," the newspaper reported in 1985. "No, his dream was simple. Reopen the dank, old-fashioned theater and recreate the mood of a generation past with tales of Western heroes in leather chaps and sultry Romeos in waxed mustaches."

The Cameo was converted into a rock-and-roll venue in 1987 for Bristol's youth. The goal was to provide an alternative place for young people to go rather than "cruising" routes in the community, according to the *Bristol Herald Courier*.

In early 1988, every Saturday from 8:00 p.m. to midnight, the venue hosted Cameo and the Country Connection with the Stateliners Band and other local musicians. Genres such as country rock, bluegrass and gospel music were showcased, plus guests enjoyed cake dancing, square dancing and broom dancing, a traditional Irish activity.

Once again, in May 1989, a local resident, Phil Parris, announced he was renovating the Cameo, and he installed a new movie screen. By the end of the year, however, local businesswoman Lois Bowie had purchased the property and announced plans to team up with a Christian organization to show family-friendly films at the Cameo.

Bowie told the *Bristol Herald Courier* that she had turned over operations to Sam Wood for him to show "clean family movies in an old-fashioned atmosphere."

Wood spent about $75,000 on renovations and received a donation of about seven hundred seats, screens and speakers from the movie theater at the Mall of Johnson City.

"The family is the key to our community, the key to our country, and I believe the key to our survival," Wood said. "I believe we need to supply an alternative for the family, wholesome, clean family entertainment."

Wood launched the All-American Family Cinema in 1990 but kept the Cameo sign. Wood also operated a similar venue in Kingsport. The new Bristol cinema opened with *The Little Mermaid* and *Life Flight*, a Christian film.

The venture lasted about eleven months and closed in January 1991. "We just could not get support from churches," Wood told the *Bristol Herald Courier*.

The Cameo remained closed for a few years, and Bowie donated the property in 1995 to the Appalachian Educational Communication Corp. Founded in 1981 and governed by a local board of directors, its mission was to further educate the region's populations "in all areas of life."

The organization reopened the Cameo in May 1997 after extensive renovations costing more than $300,000. In 2017, the Appalachian

Education Communication Corp. sold the historic building to Brent Buchanan, manager at Oakley-Cook Funeral Home in Bristol. The renovations took more than three years, and Buchanan and his team developed a lineup of live music to perform at the 535-seat venue.

"The Cameo Theatre is getting ready to rock again. In fact, it's going to rock like it never has before," Buchanan said.

The venue's signature art deco–style marquee received a whole new look thanks to BurWil Construction and Snyder Signs, according to the *Bristol Herald Courier*.

"We have completely revolutionized the Cameo," Buchanan said. "In the main seating area, we were able to save and restore the original trim in the main area."

Delayed by the COVID-19 pandemic, the Cameo reopened in 2021 and included such acts as Blue Öyster Cult, Gaelic Storm, Sister Hazel and Sawyer Brown.

Buchanan's run at the Cameo ended in 2023, and he put the theater on the real estate market.

THE PARAMOUNT

The Paramount Theatre, a grand movie and stage house, has long served as one of the Tri-Cities region's premier venues. Located in the 600 block of State Street in historic downtown Bristol, the Paramount originally opened during the Great Depression and has remained operational, off and on, for decades.

At the time of the Paramount's opening on February 20, 1931, Bristol was a bustling industrial and commercial center. The city featured a flourishing art scene with multiple venues, as well as shops and hotels. The new Paramount, an art deco–style venue, was at the center of the action.

A member of the Paramount-Publix group, which operated venues across the country, the new Bristol theater was "so distinctive a design that all visitors who have made preliminary inspections have pronounced it one of the most beautiful theatres in existence," the *Bristol News Bulletin* newspaper reported prior to the opening.

In addition, the Paramount was said to be one of the first seven theaters in the country to be designed specifically for sound picture production, the newspaper reported.

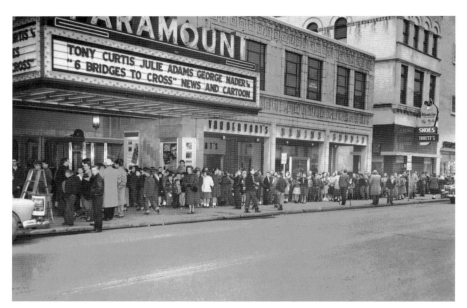

Top: A huge crowd awaits outside of the Paramount Theatre in Bristol in the 1950s. *Six Bridges to Cross*, a noir crime film, was released in 1955. *Paramount Theatre*.

Bottom: This rare photograph shows construction of the new Paramount Theatre in downtown Bristol in 1930. The venue opened on State Street in 1931. *Paramount Theatre*.

An estimated 1,400 people enjoyed the opening ceremonies, and an enormous crowd blocked traffic in downtown for several blocks. The prices were set at fifty cents for a night showing, thirty-five cents for a matinee and ten cents for children.

Opening night included a performance on the organ of "The Star-Spangled Banner," as well as a welcoming from movie star Buddy Rogers. The Paramount opened with the world premiere of *It Pays to Advertise* starring Norman Foster and Carole Lombard.

A "Talkartoon" also played at the Paramount on night one. It was a series of animated cartoons created to exploit the new technology of sound. They were released in the late 1920s and 1930s.

The Paramount's auditorium was designed with three floor sections and had no pillars to make sure patrons could clearly see the screen from any seat in the house. It was luxuriously furnished and decorated in a style that combined medieval and ultramodern art. In addition, Renaissance-style murals covered the walls.

Thousands of people are pictured visiting the Paramount Theatre in downtown Bristol for opening night on February 20, 1931. *Paramount Theatre.*

The theater also featured a state-of-the-art heating and cooling system in the basement, and it was still present in 2024. Many went to the theater just to beat the heat.

In case of emergency, the auditorium was designed so patrons could exit within three minutes, and the projection booths were fireproof, according to the *Bristol News Bulletin*. If the city's electric grid were to go down, the Paramount had its own power generator.

Visitors to the Paramount entered through the grand foyer. It featured a golden chandelier in the lobby as well as lounge rooms for men and women.

The original contractor, Meyer and Engel of Alabama, was responsible for much of the theater's construction, as well as its location on State Street. It was designed by architects McDonald and Company of Atlanta, according to a National Register of Historic Places nomination form for the Paramount, which was added in 1985.

The owners used local contractors for labor and materials, including Bristol Steel and Iron Works, Leslie Sheet Metal Works and the Central Glass Company, according to the newspaper. Officials with the Bristol Theatre Corporation owned the building and leased it to Paramount for twenty-five years.

Sam Suggs of Alabama served as the theater's first manager. Suggs "literally grew up in the theatre" and received his training at some of the best theaters in the south, the newspaper said.

"The building occupies a prominent position on State Street, adding much to the appearance of the block and, with its brilliant exterior lighting effects, becoming a focal center for all who travel the city's main thoroughfare," a reporter with the *Bristol News Bulletin* wrote in 1931.

An organist, Jean Van Arsdale, originally served as the featured player at the Paramount. She came from the Tivoli Theatre in Chattanooga and played at the Paramount three times a day, the newspaper said.

In its heyday, the Paramount also featured live performances of vaudeville shows, the big-band sounds of Tommy and Jimmy Dorsey, Charlie Spivak, Harry James and Grand Ole Opry stars Tex Ritter, Ken Maynard, Johnny Mack Brown, Ernest Tubb and Cowboy Copas, according to the nomination form. In addition, more than 1,200 children, members of the Popeye Club, went to Paramount each Saturday morning for cartoons and talent shows, the form states.

Business in downtown Bristol began to decline in the 1960s and 1970s. The Paramount's owners were not able to draw in enough patrons, and the theater closed in 1979 with a showing of *Beyond the Poseidon Adventure*.

The Paramount soon fell into disrepair. In 1981, when the building's lease expired, the property reverted to the Daniel family, who then donated it to Theatre Bristol, a local community theater company. One year later, the organization deeded the property to the Paramount Foundation, a new nonprofit. The organization spent years on feasibility plans, evaluations, fundraising and construction before reopening the venue in 1991.

Bill Price, a restoration architect, worked with Associated Construction Services from 1989 to 1991 to restore the Paramount. Images from the Paramount provide a glimpse into what took place to fully restore the venue, which originally had 1,200 seats. The entire proscenium of the stage was brought forward, which left only 750 seats, according to the nomination form.

The Paramount, featuring a grand new marquee that lit up State Street, reopened with a gala event featuring Tennessee Ernie Ford, a native of Bristol known for his country hits, such as "Sixteen Tons," and numerous television appearances.

Construction crews hollowed out the old Paramount Theatre when it was completely renovated in the late twentieth century following years of decay. *Paramount Theatre.*

For decades, residents from around the region would visit the Paramount Theatre on a nightly basis to check out the latest movies and other entertainment. *Paramount Theatre.*

One unique aspect of the Paramount is its Mighty Wurlitzer organ, which had originally been installed at the Paramount Theatre in Charlottesville, Virginia. A branch of the American Theatre Organ Society eventually acquired the organ and installed it in Bristol for a one-dollar-a-year lease, according to information provided by the theater. It was introduced to the public in 1993 with a performance of *Phantom of the Opera* by renowned organist Lee Erwin.

When the Paramount first opened, the moving picture industry was ranked as the fifth-largest industry in the country, and the *Bristol News Bulletin* estimated that twenty million people went to the movies every day. Adolph Zukor, a Hungary native, served as leader of the Paramount-Publix's company, which had assets over $60 million in 1931.

Zukor was one of the Paramount's founders. Early on, Zukor believed movies were so bad and flickered that people could hardly watch them.

Theaters were small, dirty and badly ventilated, according to the newspaper. Zukor saw great potential and believed the motion picture industry would revolutionize the entertainment industry.

Zukor began asking producers to create better movies, but they ignored him. In order to save the industry, Zukor decided to become a motion picture producer. He went on to create some of the industry's best movies in the early twentieth century.

His company, Paramount, went on to own hundreds of theaters across the country, including the Paramount of Bristol and several others in the Tri-Cities region.

A NEW TYPE OF CONSTRUCTION

Theater construction in the late 1930s and early 1940s slowed as a result of the Great Depression and World War II, according to the Theatre Historical Society of America, which celebrates, documents and promotes the structures. After the war, exhibitors were looking for ways to boost construction of theaters.

Many exhibitors turned to a structure that first debuted during the war: the Quonset hut. These are half-domed prefabricated structures made of

The Lee Theatre once operated along State Street near Peters Street and Seventeenth Street in Bristol, Virginia, nearly a mile from the central business district. *Author photo.*

corrugated steel. After the war, building permits for traditional construction materials were hard to come by and became less cost effective. The construction of Quonset huts was also faster than other types of buildings. The shape of the huts also provided good acoustics, according to the historical society.

The first Quonset hut theater was the Gaiety in Inlet, New York, which opened in 1946 and operated until 2012.

Only one Quonset Hut theater is known to have been built in the Tri-Cities region of Northeast Tennessee and Southwest Virginia. The Lee Theater opened in 1949 and featured eight hundred seats.

The venue was located in the 1600 block of State Street in Bristol, Virginia. It was originally operated by the Shelby Theatre Corporation with James Goebel serving as president, according to an article from the *Bristol Herald Courier* about the theater's opening.

The newspaper said the building was constructed of steel and concrete materials, which made it fire resistant "to the greatest degree." The exterior was covered with Tennessee Crab Orchard stone, a form of sandstone quarried in the Cumberland Plateau region of Tennessee.

Originally, the interior of the theater was blue. with other colors to create a sunrise design, the *Bristol Herald Courier* said. The front of the building was of two shades of green structural glass with polished metal trim. Clear-view glass doors led visitors into the theater's lobby.

Unlike other theaters that were farther east on State Street, the Lee had a parking lot that fit 125 vehicles rather than street parking.

The theater was originally constructed by Arthur Kingsolver, a longtime Bristol building contractor, and the marquee was installed by the Tickle Brothers sign company of Bristol.

The Lee Theatre closed after its final show on November 10, 1956. It had been owned by Neighborhood Theatres of Richmond, Virginia.

In 1957, the building was listed for lease in the local newspaper. It eventually transitioned into Bristol Lincoln-Mercury, an automobile dealership, in 1960. The dealership remained there until 1964, when it moved. In 1965, the site became home to the Pete Moore appliance store. That store remained at the theater location for decades and finally closed in 2009. It later transitioned into a furniture store, which was still in operation in 2024.

3

JOHNSON CITY THEATERS

*T*he Majestic Theatre, an early pioneer in downtown Johnson City movie history, survived decades of changes but finally closed its doors in the late 1970s.

A theater originally opened at the site in the 200 block of Main Street in 1902. It featured vaudeville and other stage performances.

The Majestic opened at the site in 1914 by Dr. J.H. Preas and several other Johnson City businessmen. The newly opened venue was operated by S.A. Lynch of Asheville, North Carolina, who later operated fourteen southern theaters.

The Majestic served as a first-run movie house for more than fifty years, according to newspaper articles. George Keys took over the Majestic Theatre in 1917 and retained the manager, George Pflamm. He operated both the Majestic and Edisonia until 1921. By 1923, Hal Youngblood had been named manager, and he retained his post until Keys died in 1936.

In the beginning, the Majestic's Wurlitzer organ was used to accompany silent films until sound pictures were introduced on September 17, 1928, when the theater presented Al Jolson's film *The Jazz Singer*.

"Nothing ever created such sensational interest before, and people flocked to Johnson City from far and wide to see and hear what was termed the marvel of the century: Movietone and Vitaphone," Youngblood later told reporters.

The Vitaphone was a sound system used for films. The soundtrack was not printed on the film—it was issued on phonograph records. The Vitaphone

Above: The site of the former Majestic Theatre in downtown Johnson City is now a park between Main Street and Market Street. *Author photo.*

Opposite: The marquees of the Majestic Theatre and the Liberty Theatre can be seen in this vintage image of Main Street in Johnson City. *Tom Roberts.*

replaced silent films. Unfortunately, the Vitaphone system was not perfect and was not always in sync, which led to laughter in theaters. The Movietone was an early sound-on-film format.

The doors opened at 1:00 p.m. for *The Jazz Singer*, and people filled Main Street—so much so that it was impossible to operate the city's streetcars through the crowd. Firemen and police officers were called to the venue to help handle the crowd, which was estimated at three thousand people, Youngblood said. A newspaperman, Carroll King, stood up on a soapbox and called off football scores to keep the crowd entertained until they could enter the theater.

Youngblood said he would often hear the audience laughing during the early talkie days when the operator did not start the record at the right time, so the sound did not sync with the film. To fix the problem, Youngblood said the operator would stop the machine, rethread the film, reset the record and start the reel over again.

The Majestic Theatre was remodeled and reopened on Independence Day in 1938. At the time, R.C. Butler, who also managed the Liberty, State and Tennessee theaters, managed the reopened Majestic. Carla B. Keys served as president of Johnson City Enterprises and owned the theater building.

The newly remodeled venue featured a luminous white front exterior, box office and vestibule. Inside, patrons entered the ultramodern and colorful foyer with a beautiful ceiling and border, illuminated by the most modern lighting fixtures, according to the *Johnson City Press-Chronicle*. Once inside, patrons found elaborate displays constructed in the theater's art shop.

The auditorium at the Majestic was illuminated by indirect light and an atmosphere of brilliant colors and designs. Navino Nataloni, a famous

Italian decorator, decorated the remodeled Majestic, according to the newspaper. Nataloni also decorated a portion of Radio City Music Hall in New York City.

The staff at the new Majestic left no stone unturned to place all modern theater equipment at the disposal of its patrons, even to the installation of hearing aids for the hard of hearing, the newspaper said. Headsets were free and could be requested at the box office. An usher would plug the set into a connection box located in the auditorium. The patron could simply control the volume to hear the film.

Four decades later, in March 1978, the *Johnson City Press-Chronicle* reported that the Majestic would reopen under the leadership of Paul Wylie, who assumed ownership. Guy McDowell, who managed both the Majestic and the mall theaters in Johnson City, said ABC Southeastern Theatres decided not to renew the lease at the Majestic.

At the time, Wylie bought the lease for a year, primarily "to keep anybody else from getting it," a spokesperson told the newspaper.

CLOSING THE MAJESTIC

The Majestic Theatre finally closed in 1981. The marquee said, "The final curtain: closing Tuesday forever." It closed with a showing of *Honky Tonk Freeway*, a film about a small town in Florida that was bypassed by a new freeway. The *Johnson City Press* later said the film's premise was similar to the story of downtown Johnson City, which had been bypassed by businesses, including theaters, going to North Roan Street near the mall.

There were efforts to save the theater, to no avail. The theater was torn down on August 11, 1993.

"I was down there today taking a last look at the grand old lady and remembering all the good times that are part of this city's heritage that took place there," said Barbara Mills, a member of the Johnson City Historic Preservation Society.

Mills said no one who lived in Johnson City during the 1950s and 1960s would ever forget "what a treat it was to get to the movies downtown." The theater also had an "extra wide, extra deep" vaudeville stage and orchestra pit in the early 1900s, Mills told the newspaper.

Following demolition, the city established Majestic Commons, a parklike area that was built at the site. Now known as Majestic Park, an urban path between Main and Market Streets, the site is briefly mentioned in the National Register of Historic Places nomination form for downtown Johnson City.

A smaller venue, the Liberty Theatre, operated in downtown Johnson City during the first half of the twentieth century. Fred Perryman, who operated a few theaters in the Tri-Cities region, opened the Liberty in 1918 at a site along Spring Street. In about 1922, Perryman moved the Liberty into another location in the 200 block of East Main Street.

The two-story brick building on Main Street had been constructed in 1916, according to the National Register of Historic Places nomination form for downtown Johnson City. The Liberty building is considered nonconforming, the form states.

The Liberty closed in 1954, and the building transitioned into the New Vogue clothing store the following year. By 2022, the building was occupied by a plant store. The former Liberty building also faces nearby Market Street, which parallels Main Street.

THE BUS STATION

A series of theaters once stood where a busy transit station now operates in downtown Johnson City. The De Luxe Theatre, the first venue at the property on Main Street near Boone Street, opened about 1922. An exact opening date could not be determined, but its building cost was estimated to be $150,000, according to an article in the *Knoxville Sentinel* on February 21, 1922.

A fire caused about $30,000 worth of damage at the theater a short time after it opened. Stage scenery and other equipment was destroyed in the blaze, which originated from a tearoom on the ground floor. The theater's piano and organ were also damaged.

W.B. McCartt, the theater's owner, told the newspaper that he would make necessary repairs to reopen the venue.

Another company later acquired the building in 1922, according to the *Johnson City Chronicle*. The new company planned to remodel the building, adding a store and business rooms on the Market Street side of the property. The remodel made the theater auditorium smaller.

In 1923, more than a year after the theater first opened, management at the De Luxe announced it was reducing ticket prices. The new prices: Adult box seats, fifty-five cents; main floor seats, forty-five cents; balcony seats, twenty-five cents; and children, ten cents.

"The patronage of the new amusement palace has been splendid and the program unexcelled," the *Johnson City Staff* newspaper reported.

The De Luxe hosted all types of events, including movies, vaudeville and political rallies. In 1922, the De Luxe hosted Congressman B. Carroll Reece, who represented the region in the U.S. House of Representatives for all but six years from 1921 to 1961.

In August 1925, Johnson City Enterprises leased the De Luxe, remodeled it and reopened the venue as the Capitol Theatre. The Capitol, which had more than 1,500 seats, was managed by George W. Keys, the newspaper said.

At intervals, the theater featured road show attractions, the newspaper reported. A veteran theater man in the city recalled that in those days, many of the shows played to capacity audiences at prices ranging from $1.00 to $3.30 per seat.

The Capitol remained open until 1931. It reopened as the Tennessee Theatre. In 1963, the *Johnson City Press Chronicle* reported about ownership changes at the Tennessee Theatre. C. Dale Johnson, vice president and secretary of Appalachian Enterprises, said his firm had purchased the interest of the Sevier Theatre Corporation at the Tennessee Theatre.

The ownership change resulted in a brief closure and remodeling, which included a vastly different façade and a large new sign, as well as seating for 1,250 people.

The Tennessee Theatre was managed by John Q. Youngblood, and the building was owned by Mr. and Mrs. Guy Carter, Ernest Carter, Mrs. Helen Carter Harrison and Mr. and Mrs. Miller, according to the newspaper. Operators closed the Tennessee Theatre in 1968, but it reopened and was renamed the Capri Theatre on November 26, 1969.

The Johnson City Press reported that the theater was remodeled, which included the installation of new carpet in the lobby, foyers, restrooms and aisles; improvements to the restrooms; a new heating system; new seat cushions, painting; and a redecorated exterior.

The Capri Theatre continued to be operated by Appalachian Enterprise; however, the company eventually dissolved, and in 1972, local theater operator Paul Wylie and his wife took control of the Capri and the Parkway Cinema on North Roan Street.

In its later years, the Capri became the only X-rated adult movie theater in Johnson City. The theater closed in 1983.

Prior to the Capri's closure, the City of Johnson City accepted an option to purchase the theater property, and officials had plans to turn the site into a municipal performing arts center. Wylie agreed to sell the property, and the city followed through and ultimately demolished the theater in 1985. The site eventually became the city's bus transit station.

THE SEVIER

Another downtown venue, the Sevier Theatre, opened in 1937 in the 100 block of Spring Street, between Main Street and State of Franklin Road.

The *Johnson City Chronicle* reported that the Sevier, which opened with *Hats Off*, was generally regarded as one of the handsomest buildings in the city. Its management said the theater was one of the best arranged and most convenient structures of its kind in the region.

The front of the Sevier featured a striking modern red design and a brilliant electric sign, which provided the theater's name in a sunburst effect.

On the inside, patrons were attracted by the walls, which were finished in light, soft tones, the newspaper said. The design was meant to be comfortable and spacious. In addition, one of the theater's most attractive characteristics was making sure that patrons had plenty of elbow room, the newspaper noted.

The auditorium featured a lofty balcony as well as walnut finished seats with leatherette cushions and resilient springs, and they were arranged so that no patron's view of the stage or screen was obstructed. The Sevier had a total capacity of eight hundred, which included a three-hundred-seat balcony.

The Sevier's management expected to host some of the best motion picture productions and independent films available, but the theater also planned to feature good stage shows whenever possible. The stage was ample to accommodate any ordinary road company, and four dressing rooms were installed.

In addition, the newspaper said the screen and sound equipment at the Sevier were the latest, most modern types available.

The newspaper reported that there was a span of about one hundred feet between the projection room and the screen. The entire building was slightly more than one hundred feet long and fifty-one feet wide, the newspaper said.

Hal Youngblood, who came to Johnson City in 1923 from Charlotte, North Carolina, managed the Sevier. During his career, Youngblood also managed the Cameo and Columbia in Bristol, as well as the Majestic in Johnson City. He told the newspaper that local men helped transform the former Elks lodge into the new Sevier. The George L. Wexler construction company completed the work, the newspaper said.

At the time of its opening, the Sevier's owner, Ray Walker, said, "I believe we have one of the nicest theaters between Knoxville and Roanoke. It is entirely fireproof, with a concrete floor and steal framework."

Despite Walker's claims that the structure was fireproof, the Sevier was destroyed by fire on May 29, 1966. Possibly arson, the fire at the Sevier was described at the time as the third major fire to destroy property in downtown Johnson City that month. The Volunteer Building was destroyed by fire on May 1, and the Johnson City Furniture Company was destroyed on May 22, the *Johnson City Press Chronicle* reported.

In 1969, the newspaper said there were no immediate plans for the Sevier Theatre site, which was in the downtown urban-renewal area. The next year, the theater company was cleared in Washington County Chancery Court regarding the company's assets. At the time, the company's stock owners were named as Ray Walker, E.R. Miller, Youngblood and the Donnelly family.

Testimony indicated that the Sevier Theatre was profitable, and the company collected nearly $60,000 in insurance benefits. The court ordered that the property and its assets be sold. In 1970, the property consisted of four walls and the foundation of the former Sevier Theatre.

Two years later, the newspaper reported that Chancellor Dayton Phillips signed an order approving the sale of the Sevier property to businessman Ray McCrary, who operated the Johnson City Radio and TV Service on Spring Street. The former Sevier was sold at public auction for $18,200, the newspaper said. The former Sevier Theatre Corporation was dissolved.

In 1976, the Peanuts Mecca Lounge opened in the theater's replacement building. As of 2024, the former Sevier site was occupied by a store.

Miller, one of the Sevier's primary associates, was heavily involved in the Johnson City theater business, according to his obituary in 1972. He spent virtually his entire life in the business and worked with George Keys, an early local theater operator. Miller also held several positions at the Majestic, the city's largest downtown theater.

Miller served as secretary and treasurer of the Sevier corporation for more than thirty years. He managed the theater for about twelve years prior to its destruction. Miller also served as president of the Appalachian Enterprises Inc., which operated the Capri Theatre, Parkway Cinema and the Skyline Drive-In, according to the obituary.

4

KINGSPORT THEATERS

ake a walk through downtown Kingsport, a planned city that is widely known as the "Model City," and one will discover a handful of former theaters, including the Strand, which was the city's first movie house. The Strand Theatre was incorporated before a newspaper started publishing in the city in 1916, according to the *Kingsport Times-News*. It was constructed at the corner of Main and Shelby Streets in downtown Kingsport. The venue showed silent pictures with piano accompaniment and a band.

It moved to the former Goodwin Furniture Company building in the 100 block of Broad Street in 1924, and its former location became the Gem Theatre.

"Built in 1915, this building has been used for everything from a country-western bar to a church," a historic marker at the Gem Theatre site states. "It was originally a movie theater that showed a variety of films including old westerns."

When the Gem opened in late 1924, the auditorium had been remodeled, redecorated and relighted. New projection machines were also installed.

The general manager of the Gem and Kingsport's Gaiety theaters told news reporters that he had contracted with Paramount Pictures and would show a complete program each day, including a feature picture, a comedy and a tri-weekly news reel.

A historic marker for the former Gem Theatre can be seen outside of a building along Main Street in downtown Kingsport. *Author photo.*

James Quillen, a former U.S. representative, sold tickets at the movie theater, according to the Archives of Appalachia at East Tennessee State University, which houses the congressman's papers. The theater appears to have closed in 1955. An article in the *Kingsport Times* in 1957 describes the Gem as a "former theater," meaning it was no longer open.

In 1994, the Downtown Kingsport Association purchased the building and later renovated it for their offices.

When the Strand moved to Broad Street, it relocated into a three-story building that had to be completely transformed into a movie theater venue. The furniture company building had been completed in 1920, and the new Strand was expected to have seating for about 1,200 patrons, according to the *Kingsport Times*.

The new venue, also known as the Nu-Strand Theatre, officially opened in April 1925 to a sold-out crowd for a showing of *A Thief in Paradise*. It was operated by Walter Harman, president of the Nu-Strand Corporation and general manager of the theater.

FIRE AT THE STRAND

Disaster struck at the Strand on December 22, 1945, when fire engulfed the venue. Alert theater employees prevented panic and possible disaster when they marshalled a full house of nearly eight hundred patrons from the theater within minutes after fire was discovered in the floor of a balcony, only ten feet from the highly inflammable projection room, the *Kingsport Times-News* reported.

For three hours after the alarm was given shortly before 6:00 p.m., crews from the Kingsport Fire Department battled one of the worst fires in the city's history.

Hundreds of spectators watched from a distance as the theater went up in flames, and fire could be seen coming from the roof.

The theater was a complete loss, but it was fully covered by insurance, the owners told the newspaper. The manager at the time, Jimmy Pepper, said Ralph Pyle, an eighteen-year-old employee who first spotted the fire, turned off his projection machine.

The Strand Theatre once lit up Broad Street in Kingsport. The Lamplight Theatre most recently occupied the former movie house. *City of Kingsport Archives.*

Pyle made sure as much film as possible was in fireproof containers and then hurried to the fire extinguishers, the newspaper reported. Other employes were alerted and began to move patrons from the theater. The fire was slow to develop, the newspaper article states, and most theatergoers left the building without panicking.

Pepper said almost 10 percent of the patrons were so little aware of the danger that they refused to leave their seats until police officers were called to escort them out.

Louis J. "Jimmy" Pepper, a prominent Kingsport promoter and theater operator, managed several theaters in the city, including the Strand, State, Rialto and others. Pepper came to Tennessee from Alabama, where he began serving as an usher at a venue.

The Strand's owners rebuilt and reopened the theater nearly two years later in the summer of 1947 with a showing of the 1946 film *Calcutta*. Several Hollywood movie stars sent telegrams to the Strand's staff congratulating them on the new movie house.

Comedian Red Skelton wrote, "Lots of luck to the new Strand." Actress Judy Garland said, "Every good wish to the new Strand," and Lana Turner gushed, "The new Strand will have a very splendid success."

The Strand remained open on Broad Street for a few more decades before closing on October 23, 1982. *Amityville II* was the last advertised film at the theater.

In 1989, the Restoration Church moved into the historic theater building, according to the City of Kingsport Archives. Later, in 2013, the Restoration Church sold the building to the Lamplight Theatre, a Christian performing arts organization.

The Lamplight originated in Fall Branch, Tennessee, back in 2005. The group performed regularly in a former music hall. There had always been hope for a bigger stage, owner Billy Wayne Arrington told local news.

With a new marquee and interior renovations at the former Strand building, the Lamplight officially opened in May 2013.

The downtown building is used as a venue for theatrical productions, dinner theater, concerts, conferences and seasonal events, according to the Lamplight's mission statement. It is offered as a performing arts center

Opposite: Longtime theater operator Jimmy Pepper managed and owned several Kingsport movie houses, including the Strand and the Center. *City of Kingsport Archives.*

This page, top: A huge crowd can be seen attending a political rally outside of the Queen Theatre in Kingsport in this photograph from the early twentieth century. *City of Kingsport Archives.*

This page, bottom: The Gaiety Theatre was one of several venues that once operated along Broad Street in historic downtown Kingsport. *City of Kingsport Archives.*

to enhance the skills of seasoned artists as well as train new actors and to cultivate their gifts and talents.

The Lamplight further expanded in 2017 with the opening of the adjacent Emporium, which features a gift shop and banquet hall.

Another building on Broad Street has been home to two early Kingsport theaters. The Queen Theatre opened in the 100 block of Broad Street near Main Street in 1917. It was operated by the Mallis Brothers, according to an article by the *Kingsport Times*.

On April 27, 1917, the Queen featured Emmett Dalton, an American outlaw who provided comments at the venue prior to the showing of three reels showing the *Double Bank Robbery of Coffeyville, Kansas*. The newspaper described the motion pictures as the first to feature any of the original outlaw characters.

In 1919, the venue was renamed and reopened as the Gaiety Theatre. The Gaiety, which was owned and operated by the Gutman Enterprises, finally closed in 1924. Later, the owners announced the building was being transformed into a store, the *Kingsport Times* said.

THE STATE THEATRE

The State Theatre served as one of the largest movie houses in downtown Kingsport and remained open for about four decades. A major renovation was underway in the twenty-first century and construction continued in 2024.

The theater is located at the corner of Broad and Market Streets in the heart of downtown Kingsport. Pedestrians walking along Market Street will discover a historic marker sign along the brick exterior wall of the State.

"This movie house on Broad Street first opened its doors on March 6, 1936, and continued showing films for the next forty-two years," the sign states. "The facility could seat 700 people and became the site of many locally produced civic and cultural events such as the Kingsport Kiwanis Club Capers. Several well-known comedians also performed here in the 1930s and 40s."

The venue, which was constructed by all-local labor and materials, was opened and operated by Kingsul Theatres Inc., a theater management company that operated several movie houses in the southeastern United States. R.B. Wilby served as the president of the company. He owned more than one hundred theaters in Alabama, North Carolina and South Carolina,

Santa Claus is arriving in his North Pole Plane in front of the State Theatre in Kingsport. The State is located at Broad Street and Market Street. *City of Kingsport Archives.*

according to the *Kingsport Times*. With an office in Atlanta, Georgia, Wilby also operated theaters in Chattanooga, Knoxville, Nashville and Johnson City in Tennessee.

The State, which was managed by Jimmy Pepper and was considered one of the most beautiful movie houses in East Tennessee, first opened with Bing Crosby's musical comedy, *Anything Goes*. The new theater's interior was described as a novelty and "something different" for the region, the newspaper said.

The interior walls and ceiling of the State were designed so it would appear patrons were in a Spanish garden. In addition, the ceiling featured an animated sky with twinkling stars and lazy moving clouds, while on each side of the auditorium one would have the illusion that Spanish dwellings surround the garden, the newspaper said. The goal was for patrons to feel like they were outside in a garden rather than inside an auditorium.

The State, which was designed by architect Earl G. Stillwell of Hendersonville, North Carolina, featured the latest in technology and conveniences, such as a modern heating and cooling system. It also included the same sound equipment that was used at Radio City Music Hall in New York City, the *Kingsport Times* said.

Also inside, patrons could check out the ladies and men's lounges, which were beautifully decorated and equipped with comfortable seating.

Stillwell designed the theater to include a screen and stage so all kinds of shows could be presented. Several vaudeville shows were booked at the time of the State's opening. The newspaper asserted, "Kingsport people are looking forward to seeing good vaudeville without having to go to nearby cities."

In 1960, the State Theatre held a grand reopening celebration with a completely remodeled venue. The theater was equipped with one of the largest CinemaScope installations in the area. Its new screen was fourteen feet high and thirty-five feet wide, the *Kingsport Times* reported.

A vintage ticket booth once stood at the outside entrance of the State Theatre in Kingsport but no longer stands at the historic theater. *City of Kingsport Archives.*

In addition, the State's auditorium was enclosed and redecorated with fireproof drapes. New carpet was also installed in the lobby, aisles and stairway to the balcony. The lobby was also enlarged, and a new concession counter was added.

"The State is the most modern theater installation between Knoxville and Roanoke," manager Clyde Hawkins told the *Kingsport Times*. "Our new marquee will light up Broad Street like Broadway. We sincerely feel Kingsport's future justifies the investment our company has made here."

The State Theatre showed its last film in 1978 and closed to the public. An article in the *Kingsport Times* said the theater's staff had expected a large nostalgic crowd of moviegoers to bid adieu to the landmark, but the seven-hundred-seat auditorium had only about thirty patrons for the 9:00 p.m. showing of *Gray Lady Down*, a submarine disaster film starring Charlton Heston.

Many potential customers decided against attending the show when they noticed a sign at the box office that announced a lack of heat, a problem that plagued the theater, the newspaper reported.

Then, in the 1980s, a Christian-based movie theater opened at the site.

Prior to opening at the former State, the Christian Cinema offered family-friendly film attractions in the Five Points area of Kingsport. In 1986, the Christian Cinema relocated to the State Theatre location, and later the name was changed to the All-American Family Cinema.

Bill Hegedus, who served as pastor of Bible Baptist Church in Colonial Heights, Tennessee, opened the Christian Cinema, the *Kingsport Times* reported.

"I was saved in a Christian movie theater," Hegedus said. That theater was in Pennsylvania and was also called the Christian Cinema. The Kingsport cinema featured seats that had been acquired from a former X-rated theater in Bristol, the newspaper said.

When the theater reopened on Broad Street it was owned by Sam Wood, who later also opened a family-friendly theater in Bristol, Virginia.

By 1991, the venue had transitioned back to the State Theatre but remained open for only a short time. It became the Top Gun Cheerleading Academy in January 1993. It served that purpose for about ten years.

In 2007, the former theater was purchased by DB3 Development Company. The company planned to redevelop the theater and obtained the original plans from the architect's archives. There were plans to reopen the State in 2009, but it appears efforts stalled.

In November 2019, Kingsport native Mark Hunt purchased the State from real estate agency Urban Synergy, according to the State Theatre's

Construction crews began working on the restoration of the historic State Theatre in the twenty-first century in Kingsport. *Author photo.*

website regarding new renovation efforts. There were some delays due to the COVID-19 pandemic, Hunt told local media.

"The plans are to restore the venue into an entertainment spot for the whole community with plans to host some live music or stand-up comedy," the website states. "We are excited to share with you the progress of the theater as we approach opening!"

FIVE POINTS

Another Kingsport venue, the Rialto Theatre, operated in the Five Points section of downtown for about four decades. The theater opened on May 26, 1921, with a showing of *Outside the Law* featuring Priscilla Dean. Managed by J.H. Gillespie, the theater was located on Cherokee Street adjacent to the Kingsport Hardware Company.

In 1934, the theater reopened after a new RCA Victor High Fidelity sound system was installed at the Rialto. The film *Love, Honor and Oh, Baby* opened the rejuvenated theater with two packed showings, according to the *Kingsport Times.*

The theater eventually became a second- and third-run theater and featured science fiction movies in the late 1950s, according to CinemaTreasures.org.

The Rialto gained a seedy reputation and eventually closed in 1961. Prior to its closure, the Rialto made the news in 1957 when all of the theater's seats were slashed, causing about $1,000 in damage, the *Kingsport Times* reported.

After it closed, the theater was gutted and converted into a billiard parlor, according to CinemaTreasures.org. In 1966, an explosion damaged the building. The owner told the *Kingsport News* that nine or ten people who lived in apartments above the AY Restaurant, which occupied the building, and a recreation hall had to relocate to area motels. In addition, the newspaper said six people in the explosion were treated for minor injuries. Kingsport's fire chief at the time said the explosion was believed to have been caused by sewer gas.

The building was demolished in 1968. Today, it is a vacant lot along Cherokee Street near Sullivan Street.

The Center Theatre in downtown Kingsport operated for less than a decade in the mid-twentieth century on Commerce Street.

The former Rialto Theatre and Kingsport City Hardware are visible in this vintage photograph. The block of buildings was eventually leveled for a parking lot. *City of Kingsport Archives.*

Pepper, who resigned as manager of the Kingsul Theatres in 1947, had plans to build his own theater. He told the *Kingsport Times* that he would open a modern, fireproof eight-hundred-seat theater on Commerce Street, across from the Inter-Mountain Telephone Company. John D. Wimberly would be co-owner of the theater, Pepper told the newspaper.

Wimberly went on to serve as the mayor of Kingsport from 1953 to 1955.

The new Center Theatre opened on January 26, 1948, with James Stewart and Jane Wyman in *Magic Town*. It was managed by the Tennessee Amusement Company, of which Pepper was president. Val Edwards served as vice president, and Wimberly was the secretary and treasurer, the *Kingsport Times-News* reported.

The Center, designed by architect Eric G. Stillwell and other members of Six Associates Inc., featured a unique rocker room. It was described as the theater's most unusual innovation. The rocker room was a glass-enclosed room at the rear of the theater and was equipped with rock-type theater chairs.

"It is for the use of mothers when their babies start to cry," newspapers reported. "The room is entirely sound-proof and children may cry as loud as they wish without disturbing other patrons."

The approximately eight-hundred-seat Center Theatre once operated along Commerce Street in downtown Kingsport. The building still stands. *City of Kingsport Archives.*

The theater became the home of the Buddy Club, which was organized in 1948. The Buddy Club grew almost to capacity membership, as indicated by attendance each Saturday at the Center Theatre, according to the *Kingsport Times*. The organization's members, which included youth from Kingsport, were attracted to the group by movies, birthday celebrations and special prizes at their theater meeting place.

The Buddy Club grew to more than two thousand children, according to the City of Kingsport Archives.

The Center Theatre was sold in 1951 and later closed in 1955. Pepper, the founder, went on to serve as a motion picture advertisement executive and traveled to theaters across East Tennessee.

The building was used as a factory outlet furniture store for many years. It still stands along Commerce Street. The theater's marquee and ticket booth no longer exist. At the rear, one can see a second-story door and balcony. When it got hot inside the theater's project room, the operator could walk on to the balcony for some relief and to smoke a cigarette, according to the Bob Lawrence's Kingsport website.

KINGSPORT'S FIRST SUBURBAN THEATERS

Two small movie theaters once operated along Center Street in Kingsport, not far from the present-day Dobyns-Bennett High School.

The first venue, known as the Hilan Theatre, opened on April 17, 1936, and featured Bert Wheeler and Robert Woolsey in *The Rainmakers*. The Hilan, which was described as Kingsport's first suburban theater and was managed by Malcolm Taylor, was located in the 2000 block of Center Street, east of Eastman Road.

The new theater served the Highland Park neighborhood, and it was housed in a building that had been completely remodeled inside and out. It featured brilliantly colored neon lights around the marquee, according to newspaper reports.

At the time of the Hilan's opening, Highland Park had been seeing fast-paced progress. Several homes and businesses were being built near the theater.

Disaster struck on Christmas Eve 1939 at the Hilan. The amusement house was swept by flames, according to the *Kingsport Times*. The fire started at the front of the building and destroyed two projection machines located in a booth above the front entrance. Firefighters were able to prevent the fire from spreading to other structures, the newspaper said.

Taylor and his family later announced that they would build a new theater adjacent to the Hilan site. The theater, which became known as the Fox Theatre, would be operated by Malcolm, Ralph and Bascom Taylor.

Malcom Taylor said the building would be equipped with all new and modern equipment and would seat 450 patrons, according to the newspaper. A new projection machine was installed, and cushion seats were used for the comfort of the patrons.

He said the theater would be similar to the Scott Theatre in Gate City, Virginia, which was also owned and operated by the Taylor brothers.

The new Fox Theatre opened on August 22, 1940, and featured the movie *Alias the Deacon*. The Fox became a successful movie house.

At one point during the theater's more-than-a-decade run, authorities raided the Fox Theatre for showing movies on a Sunday. It was said to be the first theater in Kingsport to be raided for showing movies on Sunday, which was against the law at the time.

The theater eventually closed in 1955, and the Fox went on the real estate market in 1957. The theater's marquee sign was eventually removed.

After the theater closed, the former Fox Theatre building was used as a barbershop and later a country music recording studio, which operated into the 1990s, according to CinemaTreasures.org.

A movie theater operated in the Lynn Garden neighborhood of Kingsport for about three years in the 1940s. Opened in August 1942, the Garden Theatre was in the 1300 block of Lynn Garden Drive, which had been known as the Gate City Highway.

Bluff City, Tennessee businessmen W.J. Stewart and John H. Speers operated the theater, which was equipped with the most modern of sound and screen equipment at the time in the early 1940s. It was built to accommodate 350 patrons in its comfortable and attractive auditorium.

Stewart, one of the operators, had previously managed theaters from Alaska to Florida, the *Kingsport Times* reported. At the time of the Garden's opening, Stewart was still operating two theaters in Alaska.

Action pictures, short features, comedies and newsreels, as well as other Hollywood productions, were to be shown at the new theater, the newspaper said. The venue opened with *The Corsican Brothers*.

Fire destroyed the Garden Theatre in late 1945, according to the *Kingsport News*. The site is now near a Pal's Sudden Service, a popular Kingsport fast-food restaurant chain.

5

THE TENNESSEE ENVIRONS

Outside of Bristol, Johnson City and Kingsport, the region is home to several smaller communities that have been home to historic theaters, including some of the grandest stage and movie houses in the Appalachian Mountains.

JONESBOROUGH'S HISTORIC THEATERS

A few theaters, including one that first opened in 1922 in a former furniture business on Main Street, have operated in Jonesborough, the state of Tennessee's oldest town. L.M. Broyles opened the Blue Mouse and entertained the town's residents with silent films. The theater could seat three hundred people, according to a written history provided by the Heritage Alliance.

The *Herald and Tribune* called it "one of the best equipped small-town theaters in this part of the state." Movies were offered on Tuesday, Thursday, and Saturday nights, and the first screening was well attended.

Fire struck on September 30, 1922, and damaged the Blue Mouse's operating room. It was extinguished quickly, and the theater reopened a short time later. Three years later, the venue reopened as the Lyric Theater and showcased "talkies."

The Jackson Theatre, named after President Andrew Jackson, opened in the 1950s along Main Street in downtown Jonesborough. Many locals remember taking a quarter and spending all day at the theater. Due to

The historic Jackson Theatre is located along Main Street in downtown Jonesborough, the oldest town in Tennessee. *The Heritage Alliance*

Jim Crow laws, the building was segregated, and Black visitors had to sit in the balcony.

The theater struggled in the late 1950s, and Dave Broyles, son of previous owner L.M. Broyles, tried to save the business. The Jackson closed in 1960, and the Broyles heirs sold the building in 1965.

The Jonesborough community began efforts to restore and reopen the Jackson Theatre, adjacent to the Jonesborough Repertory Theatre, in the twenty-first century. Construction work was progressing in 2024.

ELIZABETHTON'S EARLY THEATERS

The town of Elizabethton, Tennessee, experienced significant growth in the mid- to late 1920s. In 1925, Bemberg chose the town to open its first American manufacturing plant, and Glanzstoff followed suit in 1928. The German- and Dutch-financed rayon factories employed several thousand people.

With the growth, downtown Elizabethton burgeoned with new stores, restaurants and theaters.

The Grand Theatre, often considered the first movie theater in Elizabethton, opened in 1926 in the 600 block of East Elk Avenue. It had a balcony for Black patrons only, but legend has it that white men snuck up the stairs on occasion to join them and smoke cigars, according to a marker at the site.

In 1931, the Grand, which was operated by Fred Perryman, installed state-of-the-art RCA sound equipment, according to the *Elizabethton Star* newspaper.

"Dependent solely upon those who have so liberally patronized my theater in the past, I felt obligated to give them the best sound reproducing equipment available," Perryman said.

In 1934, the *Star* said Perryman was giving away two free tickets to the theater for each fifty-dollar war bond purchased at the Grand. The offer would continue for the duration of the Third War Loan Drive, a campaign that encouraged Americans to buy U.S. Treasury bonds to finance the war.

President Franklin Roosevelt called Americans to "contribute your share and more than your share" by purchasing war bonds. The drive closed on October 2, 1943, and the country reached almost $19 billion, according to the National World War II Museum.

In 1938, the *Star* credited Perryman for the "fine Grand Theatre that stands today, a credit to both himself and the fine little town in which it is located." The theater featured the "most capable efficient services" and catered to primarily western films.

In 1950, the Grand Theatre was leased from Perryman by the owners and operators of the Capitol Theatre, another Elizabethton movie house. The entire interior and façade were redecorated and redesigned, and a new screen, lighting fixtures and a marquee were installed.

The venue was renamed the Betsy Theatre in 1951, but it had closed by late 1952 for a remodeling. It then reopened in 1953 with the film *The President's Ladies*. Although it reopened, the manager said the Betsy would remain open only for special attractions and events.

A few years later, in 1957, the Betsy reopened under the management of the Johnson City–based Sevier Theatre Corporation. The Betsy closed for the final time in 1964 when the adjacent Citizens Bank purchased the building, according to the *Elizabethton Star* and deeds. Earl Snodgrass served as the theater's last manager.

At the time, Charles Burrow, who had operated the projector since 1916, remembered his time at the theater with the newspaper. The first talking picture was shown there by 1930, he said. With television and other forms of entertainment in later years, Burrow said attendance at the theater was not good.

A movie house operated at the site of the Betsy Walkway along East Elk Avenue in Elizabethton. It served as the Grand and Betsy Theaters. *Author photo.*

The theater building was eventually demolished, and in 1979, the City of Elizabethton transformed the former theater site into the Betsy Walkway. A time capsule, described in the *Elizabethton Star* as a stainless-steel vault, was bricked over in 1999 at the walkway. The site serves as a quiet walkway connecting East Elk Avenue with nearby parking lots and the Elizabethton City Hall. The site is also Number 28 on the Elizabethton Walking Tour.

The Ritz Theatre, which opened on January 2, 1929, operated in the Birchfiel building and was owned by B.W. Birchfiel. The Elizabethton newspaper said it was the most expensive structure in town. It also contained a clothing store, telegraph offices and two floors of offices.

The building was sold one month after opening for $80,000, according to the *Elizabethton Star*.

"The future of Elizabethton, with its industrial background, gives promise of many big sales and the influx of thousands of dollars of outside capital," said real estate agent R.W. Gaines, who handled the sale.

Built by the Thomas Construction Company, the art nouveau–style building features masks of comedy and tragedy and decorative patterns on the concrete façade.

Inside, the Ritz featured synchronized sound motion pictures thanks to modern Vitaphone equipment. By March 1929, under new management,

Several businesses most recently occupied the former Ritz Theatre building in Elizabethton. The building is one of best examples of art deco architecture in the region. *Author photo*.

the Ritz was seeing large crowds of people with vaudeville acts and moving pictures, the *Elizabethton Star* said.

Theater operator Fred Perryman acquired the Ritz in the summer of 1929. By August of that year, a new sign had been installed. At fifteen feet long, it was described as the largest electrical marquee in Elizabethton.

By 1955, the theater was operated by the Birmingham, Alabama–based R.M. Kennedy theater chain. It then closed in the summer of 1956, and in September, it was announced that it had been purchased by Dr. W.G. Frost and would be leased to a store, according to the *Elizabethton Star*.

On December 17, 1956, the vacant building was damaged in a fire. It eventually became known as the Ritz Mini Mall and has since housed several businesses.

Before the Grand first opened, there were a few other venues already operating in Elizabethton. In fact, a "moving picture exhibition" came to Elizabethton in May 1900. It may have been the first time a movie was played in public in Elizabethton's history. The *Mountaineer* newspaper told readers to not miss the exhibition "illustrating the highest attainment in the art of photography." The event was held in what was called the New Block Hall, a building that had been located off Elk Avenue near Sycamore Street.

"The wonderful moving picture machine will represent scenes and incidents from the late war with Spain, railway trains going at full speed,

Firefighters from Elizabethton battled a blaze at the old Ritz Theatre in 1956. The building was vacant. *From the Elizabethton Star.*

marching scenes, comic scenes, bicycle parades, etc.," the article states.

One week later, the *Mountaineer* reported that the exhibition proved to be a failure. The few people who attended and paid twenty cents said they were "disgusted" with the show.

Sometime before 1908, Elizabethton residents could see a show at the Pictorium, which was operated by Wiliam Mathis and Henry Weaver and opened in a building owned by William B. Carter, whose family has been described as the namesake founders of Carter County.

Carter's property was located along East Elk Avenue, just east of the Carter County Courthouse. A 1950 *Elizabethton Star* article on the history of the town's earliest venues said the Pictorium was "located where J. Frank Seiler's garden pool is now, at her home on Forge Street." Seiler, Carter's granddaughter, lived at the home in the mid-1900s. Forge Street has since been renamed East Elk Avenue.

The article said pictures were shown by John L. Curtis to the accompaniment of graphophone music, also operated by Curtis.

In addition to housing the Pictorium, which closed in 1914, the building also housed a drugstore and a school, perhaps the first in town. A Sanborn Fire Insurance map from 1908 shows a "primary school" along Forge Street, between the courthouse and the Carter house.

Another theater was in operation at the corner of old Forge and Main Streets, near the present-day Veterans Monument. It was owned by J.F. Grindstaff, who served as the county's circuit court clerk, the newspaper article states.

At some point during its run, the venue showed *The Perils of Pauline*, a 1914 melodrama film serial produced by William Randolph. The serial was shown in biweekly installments. The newspaper article said many Elizabethton residents remembered seeing the serial at the theater.

Soon after, the theater moved into another building that in 1950 was occupied by Benton's Confectionery. Benton's was in the 700 block of East Elk Avenue between the courthouse and the Doe River.

Part of the rent for the building was paid by three free passes for members of the Miller family, which owned the property.

Western shows were often played at the theater. "A sad thing occurred in connection with these shows," the *Elizabethton Star* reported. In 1914, a young man who wanted to be an actor was rehearsing a western act in Elizabethton. He took five bullets from a gun and laid them on the dresser. He apparently did not know that one bullet was in the chamber of the .38-caliber pistol, and he was accidentally killed when it fired while he was practicing a scene, the article states.

Elizabethton has been home to a couple open-air theaters, including the Airdome, which opened in 1911 at the site of the future Citizens Bank and adjacent to what later became the Grand Theatre.

Young boys would dig their toes into a rough wall at the Airdome, which was owned by James H. Grayson, and climb up to peep at the shows for free, the article from 1950 states. Sam R. Sells, who served as a both a state and U.S. representative, was known to speak there. He is remembered for making a fiery political speech and waving in one hand a long letter for emphasis.

In addition to operating the Airdome, Grayson also started work on the future Grand Theatre, which was Perryman eventually operated.

Medicine shows, or touring acts that peddled medical treatments for people between various acts, lecturers and musical performers stopped in Elizabethton as well. One open-air spot was located along Elk Avenue.

Elizabethton also had an opera house in the early twentieth century, the *Elizabethton Star* article states. It "was really a nice auditorium with a good stage," the newspaper reported. It was on the second floor of a building in the News Block near Sycamore Street. Stock companies performed plays, lectures were heard and local schools held graduation ceremonies there. Sells, the politician, also visited the opera house, according to a newspaper notice in 1910.

BONNIE KATE

In September 1926, the *Johnson City Chronicle* reported a handsome theater building was being constructed in Elizabethton on a lot between the Baptist church on Sycamore Street and the lot where the municipal building was located.

The church and the municipal building have since moved, but the theater remains an Elizabethton landmark.

Mrs. Ollie Browning, who moved to Elizabethton from Bluefield, West Virginia, purchased the theater's lot from A.A. Hale, according to an article in the *Elizabethton Star*.

"It is understood that the building is to be a handsome one, with arcade entrance, running in a depth of 225 feet," the *Chronicle* reported on the new theater. "Elizabethton is rapidly growing into a city, this block including the municipal building, the purposed Market House, and the theatre is one block out of the main business center."

The Bonnie Kate opened as a movie theater on May 16, 1927. The sold-out program featured a silent film.

Inside, the venue featured comfortable upholstered chairs, a stage and lights. It cost about $100,000 to build the theater, according to the *Elizabethton Star*.

A formal opening ceremony was held on July 4, 1927, when former Tennessee governor Alf Taylor was chosen to christen the theater and the Bristol Band played to a packed house. Taylor had previously served as governor from 1921 to 1923.

The Bonnie Kate Theatre has served as one of Elizabethton's premier movie houses and venues. At one point, the theater had two screens. *Archives of the City of Elizabethton.*

The film *Fate of the Hunter* was being shown at the Bonnie Kate Theatre in the mid-1960s in Elizabethton. *Archives of the City of Elizabethton.*

The theater is named after Catherine "Bonnie Kate" Sherrill Sevier, the wife of Governor John Sevier. During the siege of Fort Watauga, an early frontier settlement, she ventured outside the fort and found herself surrounded by Native Americans, according to the Tennessee Historical Commission.

"Bonnie Kate" ran toward the fort, but the gate was closed. She had a short time to escape so she ran to another part of the stockade and jumped over the top and fell into the arms of her husband, the commission noted.

Browning, the owner, lived temporarily upstairs. At the time, the building had a dumbwaiter, a small elevator for sending food or other items from one floor to another. The dumbwaiter is still hidden in the theater. Ollie Browning later died in 1933 at an apartment in Elizabethton.

"She built the Bonnie Kate Theatre and is one of the city's most beloved and popular residents," the *Elizabethton Star* said. "She had been in ill health for several months and spent the winter in Florida returning here two months ago."

For many years, Earl Bolling, another local theater operator, owned the Bonnie Kate. Others that have had their turn at the Bonnie Kate were Ray Glover and Leroy Policky, according to the *Elizabethton Star*. Bolling, who also owned two local drive-in theaters, bought the Bonnie Kate in 1950 from Bob Neal.

By 1955, the Bonnie Kate was operated by the R.M. Kennedy chain, which owned theaters in several southeastern states.

Glover owned the theater from about 1973 to 1987. Both Glover and Policky did everything at the Bonnie Kate, including selling tickets, making popcorn, selling concessions, running the movie projector and cleaning the theater between shows.

Glover and his wife, Jeanette, spent almost twenty-five years as the owners of Glover Theatres, which included the Bonnie Kate, State Line Drive-In, Jolly Roger, Flatwoods Drive-In and the Cougar Drive-In, according to Boyd Glover, the couple's son. The couple also owned Capitol Discount and Brittney's in Elizabethton.

Ray Glover's obituary said he was interested in watching movies, especially westerns of the 1930s and 1940s, going to film festivals, flea markets and traveling, including over a dozen trips to China.

Longtime theater operator and aficionado Ray Glover is pictured here outside the historic Bonnie Kate Theatre in Elizabethton. *From the* Elizabethton Star.

Glover's love affair with the Bonnie Kate began when he was a young boy, according to the *Elizabethton Star*. "I went to the movies there when I was just a kid," Glover said. "It cost nine cents to get in."

Glover later worked at the Bonnie Kate but decided when just a boy to own his own theater, the *Elizabethton Star* said. His son said he had also heard the story many times.

"I was just a boy, and Mr. Neal ran me off from the Ritz Theatre," Glover remembered. "Mrs. Gregg, who worked there, came after me and grabbed me by the arm and brought me back. My thought at that moment was 'I'd show him one day.'"

Glover's son said his father joined the army after graduating from high school, and while stationed in Germany, he received formal training on how to operate a film projector.

Theater operator Ray Glover is pictured running the movie projector at the Bonnie Kate Theatre in Elizabethton. *From the* Elizabethton Star.

Glover loved downtown Elizabethton.

"But, like the downtown, the movie industry changed," Glover said. "Big box stores and malls came in, and downtown changed. Big movie houses and televisions led to the demise of the smalltown theater."

The Bonnie Kate was twinned in the 1970s. In later years, the theater was known for its double screens, rocking chairs and buttered popcorn.

"Inside the lobby, the warm light of crystal chandeliers blended with the pale red glow of concession machines and reflection off the marble walls and tile floors," the *Elizabethton Star* said.

Throughout the years, the theater hosted talent shows, bond drives for the war and church services.

In addition to a theater, the Bonnie Kate building has housed a multitude of businesses, including law offices, a clothing store, a skateboard shop and a restaurant. In the early days, the upstairs, which has been designed to look like a small downtown, served as a doctor's office with connecting examination rooms.

In the late 1920s, the *Elizabethton Star* reported that a six- to eight-chair barbershop operated in the south wing of the Bonnie Kate.

Originally an arcade building, the Bonnie Kate's lobby once opened all the way to the second-story skylight windows, according to the *Elizabethton Star*. It was boarded up at the second-floor offices' balcony in the early 1940s for insurance purposes.

The Bonnie Kate also served as the host of the *Barrel of Fun*, a talent show that aired on the local WJHL radio station from 1938 to 1952. The *Star* reported that the program served as a proving ground for aspiring entertainers such as Ralph Stanley and fiddler Clarence "Tater" Tate. The Stanley Brothers got their first radio exposure when they appeared on the show in the early 1940s. George Simerly of Valley Forge, Tennessee, served as the emcee. More than three million people tuned into the radio show each Saturday morning.

Brian and Cindy Higgs, the last private owners, bought the theater from Leroy Policky in 2004. In addition to the theater, the Higgses operated a café and ice cream shop in the building.

Once the couple stopped operating the theater, they tried to replace it with a dinner theater and live music. The theater eventually closed its doors in November 2012 with a final showing of *The Twilight Saga: Breaking Dawn Part 2*.

The theater was de-twinned in 2014. It became a live theater venue and closed in 2015. That year, the Tennessee Preservation Trust included the

The second level of the Bonnie Kate Theatre has been designed to look like a small town with storefronts. One of the theater's signs can be seen in background. *Author photo.*

The historic Bonnie Kate Theatre is pictured without its iconic marquee in 2023. Construction crews were working on restoration efforts. *Author photo*.

Bonnie Kate in its 10 Most Endangered Properties. The organization said the theater, Elizabethton's last surviving movie house, had a deteriorating roof and water damage.

The theater then went into foreclosure before the East Tennessee Foundation purchased the property in 2016. At that point, the community began efforts to restore the landmark venue, which had fallen into disrepair. Restoration efforts have largely been funded through grants from agencies like the Appalachian Regional Commission and programs like Tennessee's Downtown Improvement Grant Program.

As of 2024, the Bonnie Kate is in the process of being brought back to become a hub of cultural and civic life.

ELIZABETHTON'S CAPITOL THEATRE

All that remains of the former Capitol Theatre in Elizabethton is a vacant lot. The theater opened in October 1949 along East Elk Avenue near the Carter County Courthouse.

The modern, up-to-date movie house was constructed by Thurman Tipton Hughes, a prominent Elizabethton businessman, according to the *Elizabethton Star*. The new theater opened with *Montana Mike*, a film starring Robert Cummings and Brian Donlevy.

Above: The Capitol Theatre operated along East Elk Avenue near Monument Circle in Elizabethton during the mid-twentieth century. *Archives of the City of Elizabethton.*

Opposite: Newspaper advertisements like this one from the Capitol Theatre often appeared in local newspapers in the twentieth century. *From the* Elizabethton Star.

"In five months, we have built one of the nicest little theaters in the country," the theater's owner told the newspaper. From the lobby to the screen, Capitol patrons would find the latest and best equipment, he asserted.

Ground broke on the theater, on East Elk Avenue between Main Street and the Doe River bridge, in June 1949. The building ultimately featured a twenty-five-foot-wide by fifty-foot-long lobby. It was described as cheerfully decorated and roomy. In all, the newspaper said it was an attractive place to wait for a friend for the next feature to start.

The theater's lounge was equipped with a California juice bar and a concession stand where patrons could satisfy their sweet cravings.

Only experienced operators were permitted to operate the Bellantyne-brand projection and sound equipment. The projectors had their own generators, in case the town's electric system had problems.

By 1955, the Capitol Theatre, as well as the Bonnie Kate Theatre, was part of the R.M. Kennedy theater circuit. The theater discontinued operation in 1958 but eventually reopened in 1966 under new management with Bob Hughes, according to the *Elizabethton Star.*

The theater's interior would include a new ladies' powder room, plus refurnished seats and new carpet. With new air-conditioning, the Capitol was one of the most modern movie theaters in East Tennessee, according to Hughes.

The Capitol then closed in 1967 and reopened again in 1968. It remained open for a few years, during which time a news headline in 1971 reported about an altercation and stabbing inside the theater.

An advertisement in the newspaper said the Capitol Theatre went on the real estate market in 1975. Eventually, the Carter County Democratic Party opened shop in the former theater.

Then, in 1979, the Capitol reopened again thanks to a group of Carter County, Washington County and Greene County businessmen. James C. Harrison of Happy Valley led the group. Claude "Tiny" Day, a sports editor at the *Greeneville Daily Sun*, was one of the owners. Day also led the Capitol Theatre of Greeneville.

"We are not here, although the majority interest is from Carter County,

TODAY THRU WED.

"You can have him... on loan!"
for a year

THE STORY OF A
Borrowed Love!

M-G-M presents

VAN JOHNSON
DOROTHY McGUIRE
RUTH ROMAN
in
"INVITATION"
co-starring
LOUIS CALHERN

CAPITOL
"WHERE FRIENDS, ENTERTAINMENT AND HAPPINESS MEET."

to put any entertainment in a bind. We feel that the people of Carter County have the right to newer and better movies, and this is our hope. Just since we started renovating the quality of movies in Elizabethton have gone up 100 percent. We hope to add to this," Day said.

The Capitol returned to the real estate market in 1981. By 1982, Capitol Discount Sales was operating in the theater building. An advertisement in December said there were roller skates, jewelry boxes, clocks, radios, luggage and tools for sale.

Disaster struck on December 21, 1983, when fire destroyed the building, which had been leased to Jonesborough, Tennessee resident Bradley Couch,

The site of the former Capitol Theatre in Elizabethton is vacant. Fire destroyed the building, which has since been demolished. *Author photo.*

who was in the process of moving antique merchandise into the building. The fire apparently originated in the back of the rectangular building, which firefighters feared would spread to adjacent buildings as they were attempting to prevent the fire from wiping out the entire block, according to the *Elizabethton Star*.

The site along East Elk Avenue remained vacant in 2024.

ROAN MOUNTAIN'S MOVIE HOUSE

The small community of Roan Mountain, Tennessee, which sits at the base of its 6,286-foot-high namesake on the Tennessee and North Carolina border, was home to a successful movie house in the mid-twentieth century.

The Roan Theatre was in the heart of Roan Mountain along Main Street, not far from the General John Wilder home and the site of the former Roan Mountain Inn.

Robert "Bob" Slaughter built and opened the theater, a traditional movie house, in 1948. Slaughter was a prominent local resident who built several homes and businesses. The theater was part of a stretch of buildings known as the Slaughter Block.

The Freeman family managed the theater with the help of the Slaughters. For many years, Myrtle Slaughter was the only person to sell tickets. Others would operate the movie projector, the popcorn machine and other aspects of the theater.

The Slaughters' daughter Geraldine said the first movie she recalled seeing at the Roan Theatre was *Slave Girl*, a film that was released in 1947.

In 1952, thieves managed to chisel their way through a cinder block wall of the Roan Theatre as they attempted to pierce through the wall of the adjacent Carter County Bank. The bank, which Slaughter built adjoining the theater, opened in 1950.

Law enforcement officials said the thieves apparently miscalculated their break-in. They were attempting to break into the bank's vault by boring through the wall between the two businesses.

Bill Whitehead, Slaughter's grandson, said that when the bank robbers hit metal, they gave up and left. They fled with about forty dollars' worth of merchandise from vending machines in the theater's lobby. Slaughter discovered the break-in and called police, according to the *Johnson City Press Chronicle*.

In addition to the bank, the Slaughter Block also included the Roan Café, a popular diner.

The Roan Theatre served the rural community of Roan Mountain for a few decades in the mid-twentieth century and was in the center of the village. *Tennessee State Library and Archives.*

The theater gained a new redecorated sign in March 1955. The local newspaper said, "It helps out considerably."

The Roan Theatre was a popular destination for local high school students. Oftentimes, students from nearby Cloudland High School would stop at the theater to see a movie. Many were said to have watched *Ben Hur*, and classes went to watch *The Ten Commandments*.

After disaster struck in December 1957, the theater became a focal point in the community. A fire destroyed nearby Cloudland High School, where 450 students were in attendance. The blaze spread rapidly through the school, but the principal, James Potter, managed to sound the alarm, and students and teachers emptied the building within two minutes.

Following the fire, Carter County school leaders devised a plan and invited students to gather at the theater. Hundreds of people met there to learn the fate of the remainder of the school year. A photograph in the newspaper shows a line of somewhat somber students walking into the venue.

Graduation ceremonies were later held in the theater in 1958 and 1959.

The theater appears to have closed by 1970. A church most recently occupied the site. The bank moved in 1973 to a new location on U.S. Highway 19E in Roan Mountain.

MOUNTAIN CITY'S THEATERS

The small town of Mountain City, an incorporated community in Johnson County, Tennessee, was home to at least two movie houses during the twentieth century.

The Strand Theatre, which was built in 1940 by Justin Rambo, was located along West Main Street in the center of town, according to the Tennessee Historical Commission.

C.B. Gowan of Inman, South Carolina, operated the Strand beginning in 1941, the *Tomahawk* newspaper said. He succeeded Cecil McHam, who had managed the venue for a few weeks. By 1945, Gowan, who brought workers with him from his hometown, had the theater remodeled, the *Johnson County News* said.

Gowan's son, Fred Gowan, was killed in action while serving in the U.S. Army in the Pacific Ocean front in April 1945 during World War II. Fred Gowan served as a manager at the Strand before he went into the army in 1943.

Interestingly, the American Legion sponsored a showing of the movie *Decision*, which explained the war department's program for the return and final burial of World War II dead. It was shown at the Strand in 1946. The film was designed to answer many questions frequently asked by families of war dead.

In 1946, theater manager Elizabeth Brown announced that the movie house would be closed for a week to install new seats and other equipment.

After the Strand closed, Courtesy Drug Store opened in the theater building, according to the Tennessee Historical Commission. A few other shops operated in the building until it eventually became the Farmers State Bank.

Downtown Mountain City has also been home to the Taylor Theatre, which opened on July 2, 1946, according to the *Johnson County News*.

"One of the largest crowds in some time will assemble in Mountain City to witness the opening of the Taylor Theatre," the newspaper reported. "The theater is not only our newest business but is in a new building erected for this one purpose and is newly equipped throughout."

Opening night included *The Well-Groomed Bride* as well as a Three Stooges comedy and an animated film in color.

Record-breaking crowds attended the Taylor Theatre in May 1947 for a showing of *Mom and Dad*, which was one of the highest-grossing films of the decade. The "sex hygiene" film included a lecturer to provide information about the subject, and nurses were in attendance to assist anyone "who may find the film more than they can take." Several patrons apparently fainted during the show, local media reported.

Because of the nature of medical sequences in the film, the newspapers reported that performances were shown to segregated audiences only. There were shows for women and high school girls and then men and high school boys.

The Taylor Theatre, which was auctioned off in 1960 and 1966, according to newspaper articles, closed by 1974. At that time, the building was demolished. The current Johnson County Bank was then constructed at the site.

ERWIN'S THEATERS

Downtown Erwin, Tennessee, a small railroad town near the North Carolina border, was home to active theaters for more than a century. The town has been home to the Lyric Theatre, Ritz Theatre, Palace Theatre, Capitol Theatre and the Holiday Drive-In.

The Lyric Theatre likely opened in 1926 on Main Avenue when advertisements for the new venue began to appear in newspapers. Like other theaters, in December 1928, during the influenza pandemic, the Lyric closed to the public. It reopened in January 1929.

The Voice of the City, a drama, was the first talking picture to be showcased at the Lyric on July 15, 1929.

In 1932, the Lyric Theatre reopened under new management. Renovations including new RCA sound equipment and a rearranged movie screen were completed, according to the *Erwin Record*.

The Lyric Theatre closed two decades later in the early 1950s. Fire later destroyed the building in 1959. The building was vacant and contained equipment from the Lyric, as well as projection units and parts for the Capitol Theatre, according to news reports. The exterior of the building had also been recently painted, and there were plans for a confectionery stand.

Another Erwin venue, the Ritz Theatre, opened in 1929 and was operated by B.M. Poe.

Poe made newspaper headlines around the region when he was accused of trying to pay two boys to set fire to his theater's competition. In May 1932, newspaper articles reported that Poe ended his theater career after he was arrested and charged with one count of attempting an arson.

The newspaper said Poe had conspired to pay fifty dollars to two boys to use gasoline to set fire to the Lyric Theatre. The plan failed when the Lyric's manager discovered the gas before the act could be committed, newspapers reported.

After Poe's arrest, the Ritz Theatre immediately closed.

The theater was renamed and reopened as the Palace Theatre. It remained open until 1935, the same year that the Capitol opened just down the street. The Palace Theatre site later became the J.B. Dick and Company, a five- and ten-cent store.

The Capitol Theatre opened along the town's main thoroughfare on November 4, 1935, with John Boles in *Redheads on Parade*. It was built at the site of the J.B. Dick and Company store before it relocated to the Palace Theatre site.

The theater, operated by the Parrott and Hendren Amusement Company, was described as not only a moving picture house but also a theater with a large, well-arranged stage, according to the *Erwin Record*. It had every modern device that could be installed for the comfort and convenience of six hundred patrons.

A wide marquee with a large neon electric sign was out front. Inside the lobby, well-lit display cases featured advertisements of coming movie attractions. The tile lobby floor was red and featured a black border. It harmonized with the "lovely tiffany finish of the walls in dull, soft colors," the newspaper said.

About 95 percent of the materials used at the Capitol were purchased in Erwin, and much of the labor consisted of local workers. W.E. Witcher served as the theater's general supervisor, according to the *Erwin Record*.

Fred Gorman, who previously lived in Lenoir City, Tennessee, was named the Capitol's first manager. He previously served as manager at the Lyric and Palace Theatres. He was largely responsible for the construction of the Capitol, the newspaper reported.

In 1935, the Pacific Film Company went to Erwin to film *Erwin in the Movies*. The film, which aired at the Capitol on November 11–12 in 1935, featured social, club and commercial life in Erwin.

Erwin, a small railroad community in Unicoi County, Tennessee, was once home to several movie houses, including the Capitol Theatre on Main Avenue. *Unicoi County Historical Society.*

The Capitol received some structural changes in 1954 to install a screen that was described as two times as wide as it was high. The new screen would be 75 percent larger than the original screen, the *Erwin Record* reported.

A second screen was added to the Capitol in the 1980s, and it became known as the Capitol Cinema I and II. It closed in December 2018 when a snowstorm damaged the theater's roof. The cost of repairs to the roof was too high for the owner, so the venue closed.

Robert Fury, a real estate investor, purchased the Capitol in 2021. He had plans to transform the former movie house into a live music venue.

"What we want to do is turn it into the best live music in the whole area, and we think we can pull really big acts, like Nashville-quality acts, here," Fury told the *Johnson City Press* at the time of his purchase.

Work on the roof did not begin until early 2024. Fury said plans for the theater were still in the design phase.

Greeneville's Theaters

Historic downtown Greeneville, Tennessee, has been home to a handful of small theaters, including both stage and movie houses.

The Princess Theatre was in the 100 block of South Main Street, adjacent to where Greeneville's Capitol Theatre was later built.

"The [Princess] is up to date in every respect, having beautiful decoration, both inside and outside, one of the best orchestras money can buy, the latest opera chairs, electric fans and four large suction fans which keep fresh air in the theater at all times no matter how large the crowd," the *Searchlight* reported in June 1915.

No town or city in the state could boost a finer moving picture theater, the newspaper added. "People of Greeneville should feel proud of the fact that they can have a few hours of pleasure every evening in one of the best theatres in the state," the *Searchlight* article continued.

At some point before 1930, a new Reproduco organ was installed at the theater.

During its operation, the theater was managed by Booth Enterprises and Crescent Amusement Company. The Princess remained open through 1937. In 1938, the former theater building was available for lease.

The Liberty Theatre opened in the 100 block of West Depot Street in Greeneville in 1919 and was managed by E.A. Booth. By 1927, the Liberty Theatre had closed and was transformed into the Palace Theatre. Prior to the Palace's opening, the *Greeneville Democrat-Sun* said no expense had been spared in making it one of beauty and comfort and a credit to Greeneville.

"The front of the theater has been decorated in pleasing effect of tan and brown and the lighting system made to harmonize perfectly with the decorations both interior and exterior," the newspaper said.

It added, "The interior walls are artistically finished in tapestry paneled effect and the draperies of silk blend into a harmony of soft shades which could only be made possible by the creative genius of an interior decorator."

The Palace, also managed by Booth, featured vaudeville, novelties and added attractions. By 1950, the Palace had joined the Nashville, Tennessee–based Crescent Amusement Company, which also operated the Capitol and Princess.

Operators closed the Palace by 1960. The building was eventually demolished in the twenty-first century as the Town of Greeneville revitalized and redeveloped Depot Street.

A building at the corner of Depot and Irish Streets served as both an opera house and a silent movie theater. Dave Mason constructed the opera house building in 1903; N.I. Howard and Humphreys Reaves, who built smokestacks in downtown Greeneville, were the original stockholders, according to historian Sylvia Bright.

The building was first known as the Opera House. It later became known as the Auditorium and then the Gem Theatre, where silent pictures were showcased.

The large brick building at the corner of Depot and Irish Streets in Greeneville has been home to several theater venues over the years. *Author photo.*

Patrons would enter through the front of the building and climb a wide staircase to the second floor, where performances were held. Bright said there was a small building on the roof that housed large equipment that allowed crews to raise and lower the heavy canvas curtains.

The second floor was about two stories high and consisted of a stage with a handsome arch, opera boxes and lots of seating, Bright said.

Bright added the Opera House featured many shows, and people even had the opportunity to watch Buffalo Bill Cody and his horse perform on the stage.

The venue closed for about ten days for improvements in 1915 when it was known as the Gem Theatre. It was also purchased by the stockholders of the Princess Theatre.

Hundreds of people visited the Gem in 1915 for a showing of *The Birth of a Nation*, a silent epic drama.

"The theater is small," the *Searchlight* reported. "Hundreds will probably be crowded, but you will be safe if you get your ticket in advance."

The Gem featured a pit orchestra, and the audience was treated to a stirring musical performance from opening frame to fadeout, Bright said. Occasionally, she said, a talkie would be featured at the Gem.

The building, which still stood in 2024, has been used for high school graduations, dances, political rallies and other meetings.

Capitol Theatre of Greeneville

The Capitol Theatre opened to the public for the first time on August 23, 1934. Architects Thomas Marr and Joseph W. Holman built the theater for the Crescent Amusement Company.

The art deco theater featured eight hundred seats and was managed by Harry Beekner. It was described as not only a talking picture house but also a legitimate theater with a large stage and utilized every device available for the production and presentation of every kind of theatrical attraction.

Located on Main Street, between Depot and Summer Streets, the venue featured a large modern marquee and a myriad of lights. Inside the main auditorium, all the seats were so arranged as to provide a full uninterrupted view of not only the screen but also the entire stage, according to the *Johnson City Chronicle*.

Opening night featured Myrna Loy and George Brent in *Stamboul Quest*. The newspaper said an interesting group of short films would also be on the program.

The sign celebrating local hero David "Davy" Crockett can be found outside of the Capitol Theatre in downtown Greeneville. *Author photo.*

Tony Sudekum, president of the Crescent Amusement Company, attended the opening. His company was one of the largest groups of theaters in the southeastern United States. Sudekum was recognized as a master showman. Beekner, the manager, previously led the Princess Theatre in Nashville.

In 1955, actor Fess Parker visited Greeneville and the Capitol for the *Davy Crockett* film, which premiered on June 8. It was the first time in Greeneville history that a picture had been shown on premier day. Parker was dressed in full leather and a coonskin hat.

Visitors to the Capitol will find a mural and an historic marker outside the theater.

"David 'Davy' Crockett was born in the Limestone area of Greene County, TN on August 17, 1786. In 1955 Walt Disney brought Crockett to the screen and renewed his Greene County roots by bringing Fess Parker to Greeneville for the movie premier at the Capitol Theatre. This colorful mural painted by local artist, Joe Kilday, depicts the 'Hero of the Alamo,'" the marker states.

Beekner died at the age of eighty-one in 1974. He had previously managed the Bijou theatre in Knoxville.

The Capitol closed in 1971. Martin Theatre Inc., which operated three theaters in Greeneville, made the announcement.

Dale D. Park, the building's owner, said the lease with Martin had less than a year before it would expire. The theater closed only weeks after the death of Beekner, who managed the facility for more than twenty-five years.

New management later acquired the building, and the Capitol reopened in 1974. It remained open for several years. Claude Day, a sports editor at the Greeneville newspaper, operated the Capitol for many years. He died in 1990.

A string of individuals, organizations and other entities owned the property for the next two decades. During the 1990s, there were fears that the building would be demolished.

Owners in the 1990s included the Park family; Christian Cinema of Kingsport, which operated family-friendly venues in Bristol and Kingsport; Lois Bowie; and the Little Theatre, according to various deeds on file at the Greene County courthouse.

During its tenure, which began in 1995, the Little Theatre hosted many shows, including plays and musical performances. The Little Theatre also launched a major renovation of the theater, which reopened in 2002. The renovations cost about $2.2 million, which left the theater company with a large debt burden, according to newspaper articles and property records.

Under the Little Theatre's ownership, the Capitol had 132 seats on the main floor and 230 in the balcony.

The Capitol encountered some turbulent times in the 2000s. The Little Theatre was unable to generate enough support to repay the loan for the renovated theater, according to news articles.

Due to those circumstances, reports said there was an attempt to sell the building. The federal government, however, foreclosed on the property in 2008 because the Little Theatre was unable to pay the debt. In 2009, the government deeded the property to Hervie Hartman, according to Greene County deeds.

Then, in 2011, Hartman sold the Capitol to the Van Allan family. Local businessman Tracy Solomon purchased the property in March 2014 as an investment into the community. The Capitol then became a nonprofit organization and once again became an active part of downtown Greeneville.

The theater's large marquee, which was dark for many years, was re-lit in 2017. The re-lighting of the marquee was the culmination of a yearslong effort and Solomon's vision.

"I bought it because it was there and it needed saving," said Solomon, who told the *Greeneville Sun* he loved theater and dance. "It was on its way to ruin when I bought it. It was literally raining on the stage and flooding in the hallway from the roof next door. It was sitting empty most of the time."

Through donations, Solomon and the organization restored the inside of the Capitol, updated the façade and upgraded the audio and visual systems. Since its reopening, the Capitol regularly hosts five-dollar movies, live events and comedy shows and supports the local theater guild.

Rogersville's Theaters

The historic district in Tennessee's second-oldest town, Rogersville, has been home to at least three movie houses. The town's first known movie house originally opened in 1914. The Palace Theatre was located on North Church Street, according to the *Rogersville Herald*. It operated in the building until 1933, when fire struck.

"Rogersville suffered one of her most disastrous fires last Friday night when three frame buildings went up in flames," the *Rogersville Review* reported. "Fire broke out in the Palace Theatre furnace room."

The Palace, Liberty Café and the Rogersville Bowling and Billiard Parlor, which had just opened for business the night before the blaze, were destroyed. Under the management of W.P. Miller, the Palace was rebuilt and reopened on February 23, 1934. The venue featured the film *Take a Chance* with Buddy Rogers, June Knight and James Dunn.

In 1936, the Nashville–based Rockwood Amusement Company opened another movie house in the center of town. The Rogersville Theatre, which was constructed by K.L. Laws, opened on October 31, 1936, adjacent to the historic Hale Springs Inn on Main Street.

The *Rogersville Review* described the new venue as "one of the most attractive and modern pictures houses." The opening featured a showing of *Robin Hood of El Dorado* starring Warner Baxter, as well as several shorts.

The owners of the Rogersville Theatre purchased the Palace in 1938 and closed it in September. One year later, crews demolished the Palace to make way for a hardware warehouse, according to the *Rogersville Review*.

On April 14, 1946, an explosion rocked downtown Rogersville and destroyed the Rogersville Theatre. The newspaper said a fire had evidently been burning inside the building before it had been discovered. The building was then shaken by an explosion that caused the roof to cave in, and in seconds, flames were shooting skyward, the newspaper said.

Firefighters were able to save nearby buildings, including the historic Hale Springs Inn and the Kyle House, but the theater was a complete loss. At the time, the theater also housed the county's public library and an American Red Cross office.

The Rockwood Amusement Company built a new, larger venue, the Roxy Theatre, at the site. It opened with a showing of *Three Little Girls in Blue* on April 24, 1947, according to the *Rogersville Review*. A second screen was later added to the theater. The Roxy had closed by 1988, when it was demolished.

The Roxy Theatre operated in downtown Rogersville. The state of Tennessee's second-oldest town has been home to several theaters. *Randy Ball.*

6

THE VIRGINIA ENVIRONS

The Barter Theatre in Abingdon, Virginia, first opened in 1933 with the idea to have patrons pay for tickets with produce. It has grown into a year-round regional theater, recognized as the commonwealth of Virginia's official state theater, with more than 160,000 visitors each year.

In June 1933, posters were placed around the small town of Abingdon proclaiming, "With vegetables you cannot sell, you can buy a good laugh," according to journalist Mark Dawidziak, who wrote and published *The Barter Theatre Story: Love Made Visible*.

The theater opened its doors on June 10 with John Golden's *After Tomorrow*. For the rest of the summer, the Barter company traveled to nearby cities of Kingsport and Johnson City in Tennessee, as well as Gate City, Chilhowie, Damascus, Glade Spring, Emory, Wytheville and Bristol in Virginia, Dawidziak wrote.

When the Barter first opened, admission was thirty-five cents or the equivalent in eggs, honey, fruits, vegetables and hams, the journalist wrote.

Saltville, Virginia native Robert Porterfield established the new theater as a regional venue after performing on stage on Broadway in New York City.

Dawidziak said that Porterfield had no doubts at the age of twelve that he wanted to become an actor, and he stunned his family by announcing his intention while breakfast was being served.

Porterfield's father wanted him to become a preacher.

The Barter Theatre has been designated the official state theater of Virginia. It is located in Abingdon and opened in 1933. *Barter Theatre.*

"You are not going into that wicked world of theater," his father said, according to Dawidziak.

After two years of college, Porterfield went to New York to attend the American Academy of Dramatic Arts. The Great Depression struck in the early 1930s, and he found himself in the same position as many Americans, out of work and broke.

Porterfield decided to return home to Southwest Virginia in 1932. He observed that farmers in the region had abundant crops but could not sell them. The Great Depression led Porterfield to create the Barter, where residents could barter goods for theater tickets.

On opening day, about 30 percent of the audience bartered their ticket, according to historical information provided by Barter staff. The concept of trading "ham for *Hamlet*" caught on quickly.

Tour guides today provide several anecdotes about what was bartered in the theater's early days. One of the first things bartered was a sow pig.

"We didn't want to hurt the pig, but it was very loud," tour guides say. "So we would tie her up out front of the theater before our shows and she served as the 'barker.'"

During tours of the history room, guests will find a photo of the pig and some of her offspring with Porterfield.

Guides also share the story of the man who brought his milk cow to the Barter. Upon receiving thirty-five cents' worth of milk to the ticket office, the person selling tickets turned and asked the dairyman, "Sir, what, about your wife?" He responded, "She can milk her own damn ticket," and walked into the theater, according to the venue's guides.

A local barber is said to have cut the hair of the actors, many of whom came to Abingdon from New York, in exchange for tickets. Another man

Robert Porterfield, who started the Barter Theatre, is pictured resting across the street from the landmark theater. *Barter Theatre.*

The Barter Theatre was originally established with the idea to allow residents to exchange produce and other goods for a ticket to see a show. *Barter Theatre.*

tried to stuff a dead rattlesnake through the ticket window. Guides say that the man convinced the frightened ticket seller, saying, "Rattlers is good vittles."

One time, Porterfield, during his curtain speech, actually begged visitors to barter anything but tomatoes, saying they'd had them every way possible.

At the end of the theater's first year, the Barter is said to have made a total of $4.35, two barrels of jelly and one pig.

"HAM FOR *HAMLET*"

Even in the twenty-first century, the theater still hosts beloved Barter Days a few times a year, when residents can bring canned goods in exchange for tickets. The food is donated to the local food bank.

The Barter also paid playwrights with Virginia hams for the rights to produce their plays. George Bernard Shaw was a vegetarian and was paid with spinach, according to guides.

World War II halted the Barter's growth in the 1940s.

Like many American men, Porterfield was drafted, which resulted in the Barter's closure. In all, 135 former Barter players served in the armed forces, according to Dawidziak's book. Four received the Distinguished Cross and two gave their lives, the journalist wrote.

Porterfield went to Hollywood in 1945, but he later returned to Abingdon to continue his work at the regional theater. Porterfield went to the Virginia General Assembly and received $10,000 in state funding. The Barter, which was declared the state theater of Virginia in 1941, reopened.

Barter Theatre staff were given all kinds of items during its early days, including chickens, a pig and other animals. *Barter Theatre.*

The Barter is the nation's longest-running professional theater and produces about twenty titles annually in world-class quality repertory. Outside of Broadway in New York City, the Barter is also one of the only remaining resident acting companies in the country.

In addition, the Barter is the first regional theater in the country to be awarded a Tony Award.

On December 2, 1969, the Barter was designated a Virginia Landmark, and it was added to the National Register of Historic Places on February 26, 1970.

BARTER BUILDINGS

The Barter anchors downtown Abingdon's historic district and now features two theaters, including the Gilliam Stage and the Smith Theatre.

The early history of the Gilliam Stage, the Barter's primary theater venue, aligns with the history of Sinking Springs Presbyterian Church.

The church's congregation had built a log structure in the early 1700s at the site of the current Sinking Spring Cemetery, about a half mile from the present-day Barter. In the 1780s, it was supplanted by a larger building, according to a written church history.

Church members later built a new church on Main Street in 1831. The Sinking Springs Presbyterian Church later sold the building in 1835 to the Sons of Temperance and built a new building about two blocks up Main Street.

The Sons of Temperance, a national organization that provided entertainment without alcohol for young people, constructed a back wall in the former church, built the stage and added removable seating for dances. The group advocated for dance, opera and theater.

During the 1850s, the building became known as the Opera House and hosted touring opera companies. According to Barter guides, opera singers would have in their contracts that they would not perform there during the summer months because the allergy season was so bad.

By 1890, the Town of Abingdon had purchased the building, and it became town hall. In 1933, the town began allowing Porterfield to use the building as the theater. From 1936 to 1941, the building was rented out to a Wild West Show.

The Barter returned to the building in 1942 but closed during the war. When Porterfield returned to Abingdon after the war, the Barter once again

Barter Theatre founder Robert Porterfield speaks to the audience before a show at the venue in Abingdon. Porterfield tried to greet the audience before every show. *Barter Theatre.*

operated in the town's building for the well-being of its residents. The town owns the building and rents it to the Barter for two dollars a year.

For many years, the town also used the building as a fire station. Until 1994, a fire alarm was stationed on the roof of the Barter and sounded as needed. When the fire siren sounded during Barter performances, the actors were instructed to freeze their position on stage and resume the action when the alarm concluded, according to Barter guides.

EMPIRE

In 1953, the Barter's Porterfield learned that the Empire Theatre in New York City was slated for demolition. He was given one weekend to remove furnishings and equipment for use at the Barter.

Porterfield took twelve men and six trucks from Abingdon to New York, where they savaged what they could with the help of the director's actor friends on Broadway. They took about $75,000 worth of goods, including seats, portraits, carpet, wallpaper and light fixtures. Many of the items have since been replaced with similar-looking items.

A lighting board from the Empire, which had been designed by Thomas Edison in 1894, was taken to the Barter's Smith Theatre.

As it originally was for a church, the building's balcony was constructed in a *U* shape and extended all the way to the proscenium wall at the stage. During renovations, the arms were shortened, and two boxes were installed.

Guides take visitors to many unique sections of the Gilliam Stage building, including the trap room, which is under the apron of the stage. In the 1930s, Porterfield didn't have any control of the area behind the pit, and the trap room was used as the local jail. The inmates figured out when the kissing scenes were planned and they would hoot, holler and bang on the underside of the stage.

The trap room later transitioned into the local animal shelter for wild animals, which also became distracting to performers. Porterfield finally gained control of the trap room, which allows for the placement of trapdoors on the stage, after World War II. It doubles as a storage area.

THE TUNNEL

Other than the stage, the Barter's hidden tunnel may be the theater's most notable attraction. During tours, guides will take visitors to a storage area used for lighting and sound equipment. But at the back of the room, visitors will discover a tunnel that once connected the Barter with the nearby Martha Washington Inn.

During war, it was uncouth to attack or burn a hospital, so the inn became a hospital. The Martha's first floor was a hospital, but the upper floors were used for Confederate ammunition storage.

It's unknown how the tunnel originated, but it was used to smuggle guns and ammunition between the two properties.

Guides say the Union army discovered the tunnel, and two Confederate soldiers were shot and killed inside while smuggling ammunition. The tunnel collapsed in the 1890s, leaving one ghost on the Martha side and another on the Barter side. The legend is that the ghost is never seen, but a hostile, unseen presence is there and never felt past the door, guides say.

During renovations in 1996, three carpenters were on their break at 3:00 a.m. and were apparently spooked by the ghost. They got up and ran, left the room and refused to return, according to guides.

Barter's Smith Theatre, previously known as the Barter Playhouse and Barter Stage II, was constructed in 1829 as a Methodist church. After a fire in 1914, only the main building of the church remained standing, according to a written history from the Barter. The building has also been used by the nearby Stonewall Jackson College and Martha Washington College as a gymnasium and a storage area.

In 1961, the building was renovated by Barter Theatre as a small theater, with major improvements made in 1973 and again in 1985, according to the Barter.

WHO'S WHO OF BARTER

The Barter has served as a steppingstone for a who's who of actors and actresses, including Ned Beatty, Will Bingham, Ernest Borgnine, James Burrows, Gary Collins, Hume Cronyn, Frances Fisher, Wayne Knight, Larry Linville, Gregory Peck and Patricia Neal.

Peck, who went on to win an Academy Award for his portrayal of Atticus in the movie version of *To Kill a Mockingbird*, served as a Barter props intern in the late 1940s. His job was to drive around town, look into people's windows, knock on their door and ask if the theater could borrow things like a coffee table for productions, according to the Barter.

He eventually got to act when the Barter was up the street at its production building. A newspaper review of the play said, "Gregory Peck is really going to be something."

Neal, a native of Knoxville, Tennessee, was a Barter apprentice in 1942, according to a *Roanoke Times* article. Four years later, she received a Tony Award for her role in *Another Part of the Forest*.

The actress, who was born in Kentucky, was quickly signed by Warner Brothers and made thirteen movies in four years, including *John Loves Mary*, *The Hasty Heart*, *The Fountainhead* and *Operation Pacific*, according to the *Times*. Neal, who often returned to the Barter, won an Academy Award for her performance in *Hud*.

Neal's Barter credits include *Letters to Lucerne*, *No Boys Allowed*, *The Man Who Came to Dinner*, *There's Always Juliet* and *French Without Tears*.

"It really launched her career," said former Barter director Richard Rose of Neal's one year at the theater.

The Barter has had only four artistic directors, including Porterfield, who died in 1971 and was recognized by the likes of President John F. Kennedy,

Lady Bird Johnson and Eleanor Roosevelt; Rex Partington, a former Barter actor who served as director from 1972 to 1992; Rose, 1992 to 2019; and Katy Brown.

Porterfield, the first director, was also friends with Tennessee Williams, who wrote his play *The Milk Doesn't Stop Here Anymore*, on the steps of the Martha Washington Inn across the street.

Opposite: The Barter Theatre is the longest-running professional theater in the United States and typically produces about twenty titles a year. *Barter Theatre.*

This page, top: The repertory theater company at the Barter often travels around the region to provide entertainment at schools, businesses and other theaters. *Barter Theatre.*

This page, bottom: Actors and actresses can prepare for shows with makeup and costume directors in dressing rooms at the Barter. *Barter Theatre.*

THE PANDEMIC

The COVID-19 pandemic drastically affected the world's theater industry. In March 2020, the Barter announced that it would postpone the opening of *Macbeth*, *Driving Miss Daisy* and *Peter Pan*, which were originally scheduled for March 26, April 2 and April 7, respectively. The decision was made in response to Virginia governor Ralph Northam's ban on large gatherings and to ensure the safety of the Barter's staff, volunteers and patrons, according to a news release from the theater.

As a result, the Barter began filming the productions for future streaming to patrons. The theater eventually launched Barter on Demand.

During the pandemic, Katy Brown, the producing artistic director at the Barter, drove around town, looking for outdoor venues. She came across the Moonlite Drive-In on the edge of town. Brown had the idea to construct a stage where actors could perform and be filmed live, projected on the big screen, and audiences could stay inside or sit outside of their cars and hear the show live through their radios.

The Barter produced twelve shows and four original concerts from July 2020 to December 2021 at the Moonlite.

"During the height of the pandemic, we were able to safely give the people of our region a great one-of-a-kind theatrical experience," the Barter said in a written statement.

The Barter Theatre revitalized the old Moonlite Drive-In during the COVID-19 pandemic to provide entertainment for socially distanced audiences. *From the* Bristol Herald Courier.

In 2020, the Barter sold 21,800 tickets at the Moonlite, Brown said. The theater sold even more tickets during 2020 with a touring show prior to the pandemic, plus streaming performances from the main stage.

"Overall, we served 70,000," Brown told the *Bristol Herald Courier*. "As pandemic numbers go, it's pretty exciting."

In a normal year, the theater sells 145,000 in-person tickets, she added.

ZEPHYR THEATRE

The Zephyr Theatre opened on Tuesday, November 21, 1939, in Abingdon. Invitations were mailed to select residents for opening night by the Lincoln Theatre Corporation in nearby Marion, Virginia, which developed and operated the new venue. Construction of the new movie house, which was in the 200 block of Main Street, between Russell Road and Cummings Street, cost about $55,000 at the time of its opening.

Abingdon's new movie house was named after the Lincoln Zephyr, a line of luxury cars that was produced by Ford from 1936 to 1942.

Nearly two years after its opening, the Zephyr Theatre was extensively damaged by fire.

"Abingdon's most disastrous fire in many years occurred at 3:15 p.m. Tuesday when the Zephyr Theatre was gutted by flames," the *Bristol News Bulletin* reported.

Firefighters from nearby Bristol were also called to the scene to help prevent spread of the blaze to adjoining structures, the newspaper reported. About twenty-five people were inside the Zephyr when the blaze was discovered. The patrons made an orderly exit, but Louis E. Stone, manager of an adjacent store, suffered minor burns to the face and hands. The newspaper said Stone was injured while helping Dorothy Dennison, the theater's box office clerk, escape from the building.

The theater was completely gutted by the fire, seats were burned beyond repair and a portion of the walls fell, the newspaper said. The roof of an adjacent store was also damaged.

Interestingly, the newspaper reported that D.D. Query, the general manager of the Lincoln Theatre in Marion, was tried in circuit court at the time on a charge of violating a city ordinance by operating the Abingdon theater on Sunday.

The town's mayor, Tom Phillips, assessed a fine of $2.50 at a previous hearing, and a jury convicted Query and fixed a fine of $5.00.

The Zephyr Theatre in downtown Abingdon once featured a large marquee sign showcasing the day's attractions. *Charlie Barnette.*

After the fire, the Zephyr was rebuilt and reopened in late 1941.

During its early days, it was said that "you could get your movie ticket, popcorn, peanuts, and a bottle of soda for 50 cents," according to the owners of the Zephyr Antiques store, which has recently occupied the building.

The theater became part of the Query Enterprises chain in the early 1960s and appears to have closed in the early 1970s.

GATE CITY'S THEATERS

The Boone Theatre of Gate City opened along Jackson Street in downtown Gate City in July 1936. Dick Suggs, who was described as a "showman with wide experience," said he had leased the property and would provide the area with a "high type of picture shows," according to the *Kingsport Times.*

The new Boone featured modern sound and projection equipment, the newspaper said. The movie house showcased films every Sunday. Advertisements for the Boone appear to have ended in 1937.

Another theater opened in the summer of 1938. "Gate City left the ranks of towns without a first-class theater tonight with the formal opening of the Gate City Theatre, under the management of J.H. Murphy," the *Kingsport Times* reported.

The new venue was constructed by Ryland G. Craft, a former Virginia state senator, and was leased by Murphy, who had also operated a chain of theaters in Wise County.

In addition, another theater was being constructed by Dr. B.K. Barker, a local dentist, in downtown Gate City. At the time, the newspaper said the new venue would be called the Boone Theatre, but it appears to have opened as the Scott Theatre in July 1938.

The new Scott, which was owned by brothers Ralph and Bascom Taylor, featured a grill room and a roof garden, which was described as the only one within a one-hundred-mile radius of Gate City.

On opening night, the Scott was full, and management had to turn away about three to four hundred people. The theater featured *Golden West Cowboys* starring Gene Autry.

In 1941, the original Gate City Theatre was destroyed by fire. Responding first responders were able to save the nearby Gate City Motor Company, as well as the Scott Theatre.

The fire was first spotted at 11:45 p.m., about an hour after the final movie showcase of the evening. "Had it occurred an hour or two earlier the fire that destroyed the Gate City Theatre here late last night might have burned several to death," the *Kingsport Times* reported.

Several movie houses have operated along Jackson Street in downtown Gate City, including the two theaters pictured here. *Scott County Virginia Historical Society.*

The Gate City Theatre, which was operated by the Lincoln Theatre Corporation, reopened in June 1942. The new venue building was owned by R.G. Craft and was constructed with "an eye toward beauty, convenience, and comfort," the newspaper said.

The building was completely fireproof and had a seating capacity of 485. The newspaper said the new theater had a large balcony for "colored patrons."

Another Gate City movie house known as the Taylor Theatre opened in April 1948. The Taylor brothers operated the venue. It had a capacity of 750 patrons and was decorated in a rose and beige motif, according to the *Kingsport Times*. It also had fireproof fabric panels.

In the basement, female patrons could visit the large ladies' powder room and men could enjoy the smoking room. The two rooms were in the basement to free up space in the lobby, the newspaper said. A full soda shop and a grill were located at the theater's entrance.

The Taylor, which was in the 100 block of Jackson Street, opened with *April Showers* starring Jack Carson and Ann Sothern, the newspaper said. The theater went on to become popular for western and family films.

For at least five years, the town of Gate City had three operational movie houses open along Jackson Street. Advertisements for showings at the Gate City Theatre appear to have ended in the mid-1950s. The Scott Theatre, which was located near to Quillen Hardware, was razed by flames on March 4, 1956, according to the *Bristol Herald Courier*. The Taylor closed during the early 1960s.

Other Southwest Virginia Theaters

The town of Saltville, which was named for the salt marshes in the area, has been home to three theaters during its history, according to Don Smith, a local photographer and historian. Smith said the Pleazu was probably built about 1910 and was where the town hall is located.

The Victory Theatre was built in 1922, but it closed when the Salt Theatre opened in 1949. The Salt, which was operated by multiple organizations, including Field Theatres and Query Enterprises, closed in the 1960s. After its closure, the Victory eventually transitioned into a bank. The Salt Theatre site is now home to the Museum of the Middle Appalachians, according to Smith.

The town of Chilhowie was home to both a historic theater and a modern venue. The State Theatre operated in downtown Chilhowie and was managed by Query Enterprises in the 1950s and 1960s. In 2000, the independently owned Lee Theatre operated in Chilhowie. It stayed open for more than a decade.

The Dixie Theatre operated in the early twentieth century in the town of Glade Spring, a small railroad community. The theater opened in a building in the town square.

A couple movie houses have operated in the town of Damascus, which is located at the crossroads of the Appalachian Trail and the Virginia Creeper Trail. The Star Theatre appears to have been open in the early twentieth century. In 1937, the *Bristol Herald Courier* reported that a new 450-seat theater would be managed by Sam Hendricks. The State Theatre later operated in Damascus.

The historic Lincoln Theatre, which first opened in 1929, is in downtown Marion. The venue, which features art deco and Mayan Revival architecture, has been home to the *Song of the Mountains*, a long-standing music program.

The town of Lebanon is home to the Russell Theatre, a venue first established in 1938. It has served as a movie house and a club for teenagers, and in 2023, it opened as a dramatic theater and live performance venue.

COAL TOWN THEATERS

A history of the Tri-Cities region would be remiss to not include the strength and influence of the coal industry of Southwest Virginia. The coalfield communities have depended almost exclusively on mining for their economic base for more than a century. After all, rich coal seams can be found in seven counties in Virginia, cradling the Kentucky and West Virginia borders.

During the early twentieth century, coal companies established small towns to house their employees. The communities of Dante, Derby, Dunbar, Exeter, Osaka, Pocahontas and Stonega were founded and thrived for decades as company towns.

The coal companies provided everything that their employees needed, including homes, churches, schools, post offices, a commissary, law enforcement and entertainment and recreation venues.

One of those communities, Stonega, was the largest company town built by the Virginia Coal and Iron Company. The camp was originally established in 1895 just north of the town of Appalachia in Wise County. It was owned and operated as a company town until the 1950s.

Like other coal towns, the community of Arno in Wise County, Virginia, had its own movie theater. *Southwest Virginia Historical Museum.*

Many towns, including Stonega, had their own band, scout troops, athletic teams and theaters.

In 1916, the Stonega company added a theater in the community, which had about 2,470 people, according to the National Register of Historic Places. Officials had begun converting buildings for use as theaters and had observed in the previous year that "people living at the plants where we have built theaters and equipped them with moving picture apparatus have appreciated them."

Coal company leaders also recognized a need to provide a positive environment for workers in the light of labor conflicts and labor shortages during World War I. A Stonega report in 1916 used the phrase *contentment sociology*. The Stonega company said, "Contentment is necessary for the stability of labor and prevention of unions and lockouts. Playgrounds, amusement halls, night schools and domestic science classes have been carefully worked out for the benefit and contentment of the employee and his family."

The modern Stonega theater showed the latest movies and hosted live performances as well. In addition, theaters often also served as dance halls and meeting venues.

Life in the coal towns began to change in the 1950s. By the 1960s, hundreds of thousands of miners had left the coalfields of the region and the coal camps were obsolete. Many buildings at Stonega, Osaka, Arno and Roda stood vacant.

As town functions ended in Stonega in 1952, the company abandoned many of its community features. The town store and theater at Stonega were demolished.

Other coal towns in the region also had theaters, including Derby and Exeter, which featured architecture like the venue in Stonega. Those theaters have also been demolished.

Some of the larger towns in the region served as commercial and entertainment centers. The town of Appalachia, Virginia, was home to two movie houses: the State Theatre, which originally opened as the Cumberland Theatre, and the Appalachian Theatre. The two venues, which no longer exist, showed double-feature movies that drew clientele from Big Stone Gap and Norton via daily trains, according to the National Register of Historic Places nomination form for Appalachia.

Another brick-and-steel theater was constructed but never opened, according to the nomination form.

Several historic buildings remain intact in downtown Appalachia, including the former M.D. Collier Furniture Store building housing the Appalachia Cultural Arts Center, which hosts theatrical, musical and historical programs.

The town of Big Stone Gap, Virginia, was home to the Amuzu Theatre, which later became the Big Stone Gap Theatre; the Earle Theatre; and the Trail Theatre. Norton, Virginia, once was home to the Lyric Theatre, Bolling Theatre and the Koltown Theatre.

More recently, the Park Avenue Theater opened in downtown Norton. From 1995 to 2009, the venue hosted the VA-KY Opry. It screens movies and hosts other events and features a new lobby and concession area. Norton is also home to a modern multiplex. The nine-screen Cinema City opened on Coeburn Avenue in 2008 at the site of a former Piggly Wiggly grocery store.

The town of Coeburn, Virginia, which saw a building boom in the mid-twentieth century, has also been home to a few theaters, including the Star Theatre on High Avenue and the Coeburn Theatre on Front Street.

The town of Big Stone Gap, Virginia, had several movie theaters, including the Big Stone Gap Theatre. *Southwest Virginia Historical Museum.*

Nearby St. Paul, Virginia, is home to the historic Lyric Theatre, which originally opened as a movie house in 1953 and has since transitioned into a performing arts center. The town's theater history includes the Gaiety Movie Theatre, which opened in the early 1920s on Fourth Avenue, according to the National Register of Historic Places form for the St. Paul Historic District. The owners of the Gaiety then built the Cavalier Theatre on Broad Street. In what the form calls an aggressive competitive move, William A. Turner then built the Lyric across from the Cavalier in 1950.

Tragedy struck in November 1954. The Cavalier's owner fell from a ladder while preparing for a show at the Lyric Theatre. In 1959, the man's widow sold the Cavalier to Fred Phillips, who chose to remodel the building for use as professional offices and apartments, according to author Jerry Couch.

The Lyric remained open through the 1980s, and the building began to deteriorate. The marquee eventually collapsed.

In 2013, the Town of St. Paul purchased the former Lyric Theatre building and launched a $4.75 million project to reopen the venue. Funding was used to re-create some of the old theater's seating and build new meeting spaces, according to the *Kingsport Times-News.*

Inside, the theater balcony overlooks the stage and the ground-floor seating for about two hundred people. The Lyric reopened in 2023 as a performing arts theater.

The small town of Pennington Gap in Lee County has been home to a world-class theater since 1947, but it has not always been open. A few decades after it opened in 1947 along Morgan Avenue in the community's downtown area, the Lee Theatre closed in the mid-1970s.

Since that time, it has been carefully restored by the Town of Pennington Gap and reopened in 2013, according to the theater's website.

The town of Dryden, another Lee County community, was home to a modern movie house in the late twentieth century. The Lee Cinema opened in 1980. It was remodeled in 2002, according to CinemaTreasures.org. Dryden's lone theater later closed in 2009.

7

DRIVE-IN THEATERS

The mid-twentieth century, especially the decades after World War II, brought drive-in theaters to the Tri-Cities region of Northeast Tennessee and Southwest Virginia. "Modern" and "well-conducted" drive-in theaters built by the 1950s were "not a fad or passing fancy," but an amusement institution catering to families, especially popular with young married couples with children too young to take to a conventional theater, according to an article published in the *Elizabethton Star*.

The drive-in concept was invented and patented by Richard Hollingshead Jr. in 1933, according to a National Register of Historic Places nomination form for the Moonlite Drive-In, which is located near Abingdon, Virginia. There were some more primitive drive-in theaters that were established back in the 1920s, but those primarily showed silent films.

A lover of both movies and cars, Hollingshead opened the first drive-in that year in Camden, New Jersey. Hollingshead created the venue as a solution for people unable to comfortably fit into smaller movie theater seats after creating a mini drive-in for his mother, according to the New York Film Academy. Appealing to families, he advertised the drive-in as a place where "the whole family is welcome, regardless of how noisy the children are."

At the time of Hollingshead's theater, there were no such things as in-car speakers. Patrons would listen to the sound over a series of large outdoor horns, the *Elizabethton Star* said. Eventually, drive-in operators placed a small horn on a post between two cars to provide sound. It provided sound, but there was too much echo and distortion and the quality was poor.

By 1941, RCA had introduced in-car speakers that could provide satisfactory sound for patrons. Each visitor could control the volume and reduce noise pollution.

After Hollingshead established his drive-in theater, it took several more years for the idea to catch on across the country. By 1946, there were only 102 drive-in theaters in existence, according to the Moonlite nomination form.

Drive-in theaters soon, however, became part of a boom in drive-in businesses during the post–World War II era. The boom was spawned by affordable and more available automobiles. Drive-in restaurants also became popular, the nomination form states.

In 1949, there were 820 drive-in theaters nationwide.

Drive-in theaters had long served as old-style cow pasture movie theaters, appealing principally to necking parties, and in many cases, they were no more than just licensed lovers' lanes, the *Elizabethton Star* said in 1953. The venues transitioned into modern, convenient theaters for the whole family.

KING SPRINGS DRIVE-IN

Local theater operator Bernie Wylie opened the region's first drive-in theater in Johnson City. The King Springs Drive-In was located along present-day King Springs Road between Milligan Highway and Tennessee State Route 91.

In 1940, when the venue opened, it was considered one of the first five drive-in theaters in the world, according to the *Johnson City Press Chronicle*. It opened with the film *Romance of the Limberlost*.

The novel theater resembled a park. The only trees that were cut were those that interfered with the view of the drive-in's screen or with parking, according to an article on local drive-ins published in the Johnson City newspaper in 1985.

Wylie's drive-in was small by comparison to later drive-ins. During the summer, patrons were comforted by large fans that had been placed on tall stands at the ends of each row of cars. Due to the parking stall walls, the breeze from the fans was practically lost. Speakers were built inside each space and could be heard through an open car window.

Admission was free for the first three days at the King Springs Drive-In, and the local newspaper advertised, "Free Movies in Your Car!"

Wylie, who built the theater, saw his first drive-in theater on a trip to New Orleans. He became involved in every Johnson City drive-in except the Family Drive-In on West Market Street.

In the late 1940s, Wylie formed a partnership with Charlie Fain to open the Tri-City Drive-In at a site in northern Johnson City. Shortly afterward, Wylie and Roy Fawcett built and opened the Twin City Drive-In, between the cities of Elizabethton and Johnson City.

Johnson City's Drive-In Theaters

The King Springs, Twin City and Tri-City venues were built with private stalls, which were banned in the 1950s. As a result of new laws banning the walls, the King Springs Drive-In closed. The walls at the Tri-City and Twin City were partially cut down, according to the *Johnson City Press-Chronicle*. The venues remained open for only a few more years as more modern drive-ins began to attract visitors.

The Twin City and the Tri-City venues were demolished and redeveloped. The site of the Tri-City Drive-In, which was located at the fork of the Kingsport and Bristol highways, has since become an automobile dealership.

Paul Dailey, who owns the former Twin City site, has built a home on the property. It is located near the intersection of Route 91 and Dave Buck Road. When he purchased it, Dailey said he had no idea a drive-in had been located on the land.

"We didn't find anything except a bunch of old buried wires running all over the property," Dailey said. "I assume they were for the speakers. Most of what we found or dug up was garbage that Smith Mobile Home left behind or buried."

The mobile home dealership operated on the Twin City site years after the drive-in closed.

Robert "Bob" Neal and Dick Kennedy opened the Family Drive-In of Johnson City in the early 1950s along West Market Street. It had a capacity of about five hundred cars and featured a patio for walk-in customers and a children's play area. The theater opened with *The Quiet Man*, featuring John Wayne.

A few years later, Wylie opened the Skyline, which was more than a mile west along Market Street. During opening weekend, the Skyline showcased the movies *The Outcast* and *The Long Wait*, according to CinemaTreasures.org.

A Walmart big-box store and other businesses occupy the site of the former Skyline Drive-In of Johnson City. *Author photo.*

The two theaters heavily competed against each other. In a 1955 advertisement, the Family said, "We have the biggest screen in Johnson City!" In response, a Skyline advertisement said, "Only Giant Screen in Johnson City!"

Wylie died in 1957 and left the Skyline to his three daughters and son, Paul Wylie, who went on to operate several local movie houses. Another theater operator, E.R. Miller, purchased the sisters' interest in the Skyline, the *Johnson City Press-Chronicle* said.

The Skyline Drive-In remained a successful theater for years. Cars often filled the parking spaces. Paul Wylie told the newspaper that he remembered a showing of *Thunder Road* that led the theater to stretch capacity from about three hundred cars to about five hundred.

As a result, several police officers had decided to park their cars at the theater. During the movie, the newspaper said officers trying to leave found it difficult to exit the packed lot.

Wylie joked, "It would have been a great night to rob a bank," the *Press-Chronicle* reported.

The Family Drive-In closed in the mid-1970s, leaving only the Skyline to remain in operation in Johnson City.

In late 1977, it was reported in the *Johnson City Press* that a construction company sued three Johnson City men regarding a potential breach of contract to establish a shopping center, known as Westland Center, at the Family Drive-In site. It was supposed to house a supermarket and drugstore. The Family site was located where a Mexican-style restaurant operates, as well as parking for nearby medical offices.

The Skyline Drive-In eventually began to attract fewer and fewer customers as the decade progressed.

Finally, the Skyline closed in March 1984, when a fire destroyed the concession stand, projection room and Wylie's home, all of which were housed in the same building at the venue. Wylie had just left the property about a half hour before the fire started, according to the *Johnson City Press*. Prior to the fire, the Skyline last showed a movie in October 1983.

Wylie later said he believed local drive-in theaters closed due to smaller, less comfortable cars that followed the 1972 rise in gas prices.

The Skyline property remained vacant for years. The property has since transitioned into a large commercial development and features a Walmart store, a car wash and other stores and restaurants.

ELIZABETHTON'S DRIVE-INS

At least two drive-in theaters have operated in Elizabethton, Tennessee, including the Stateline, which remained in operation as of 2024. The Stateline opened in 1947 along U.S. Highway 19E in the Valley Forge community. It has always featured one screen and has a capacity of 250 cars. The Stateline continues to remain open from April through September.

The landmark theater formally opened its snack bar in 1952, according to an article in the *Elizabethton Star*. It is housed in a block building and was fitted with a loudspeaker to let patrons know when their food was ready. In addition, the concession stand had a modern grill and fountain.

"I am glad to give these new conveniences to my customers, and hope to continue serving all of you with the best in movie entertainment as in the past," said Stateline owner Earl Bolling. "For an evening of entertainment and relaxation, come up early, have supper and see a good show."

Like other concessions, the Stateline featured popcorn, candy, snow cones, chicken, French fries, soft drinks and all kinds of sandwiches. Patrons could also purchase cigarettes and cigars.

Bolling, who came to Elizabethton from Norton, Virginia, purchased the drive-in in July 1950.

The Stateline Drive-In of Elizabethton is one of the longest-running drive-in theaters in the Tri-Cities region. *Author photo.*

In 1973, another Elizabethton theater operator, Ray Glover, took over management of the Stateline Drive-In. During Glover's time, he designed and installed the marquee at the drive-in. His son said Glover was inspired, in part, by a marquee he saw on a trip to either Nevada or California.

Before the four-lane U.S. Highway 19E was constructed, visitors to the drive-in theater would enter from Stateline Road, according to Glover's son.

Andrew Wetzel, an Elizabethton firefighter, and his wife purchased the Stateline in 1996. Neither had prior experience in theaters or small business, they told WJHL-TV.

Throughout their ownership, the Wetzels have been concerned about the future of the drive-in business, which they said has been steady at the Stateline.

In 2014, the Elizabethton community and the entire region rallied together to vote on the theater to receive a new digital movie projector, a move that saved the Stateline. Project Drive-In, Honda's national effort to help save drive-in theaters facing closure due to the end of 35mm film distribution, awarded venues across the country, including the Stateline. More than 2.6 million online votes determined the total of nine winning theaters, according to Honda, an auto manufacturer.

"It's not often that a company gets the opportunity to help preserve an American pastime," Honda and Acura's social marketing manager, Alicia

Jones, said in a news release in 2014. "It has been an honor and a privilege to bring national and local attention to the fate of drive-ins and to meet the passionate owners of these small businesses."

In 2012, the Hollywood movie industry started transitioning to digital cinema technology and decided to stop releasing 35mm film. The change led drive-in theaters to decide whether to spend thousands of dollars on new technology or close.

"The new projector really brought us out of the dark age," Wetzel told the *Elizabethton Star*. "We were running the same projectors that were original to the theater in 1947. They were great pieces of equipment, but they were mechanical. The new stuff is all computer based."

After the COVID-19 pandemic, Wetzel began toying with the idea of selling the theater, even asking the local government to purchase the property. The drive-in was still owned by the Wetzel family in 2024.

A second drive-in theater, the Valley Drive-In, opened in the Lynn Valley community in 1953. The new drive-in, located about two miles from the town of Elizabethton, was expected to be a highlight for residents of Carter County, especially those in the Lynn Valley and Stoney Creek area. It was located on Broad Street Extension, which at the time was known as the Stoney Creek Highway, near Bill Crawford Lane.

The new venue, which opened on August 24, 1953, was also operated by Earl Bolling. It offered the best in modern drive-in technology, including RCA sound, projection and electronic equipment, according to the *Elizabethton Star*. It also featured other conveniences that made the new venue "one of the finest recreational projects in the nation."

The giant modern screen, sixty by sixty feet, offered an unobstructed view for the theater's patrons. A total of about three hundred cars could park at the drive-in, which meant countless passengers could enjoy the show.

A large and modern concession stand at the center of the drive-in offered an assortment of refreshments and snacks for patrons. It was built of glazed tile block and offered adequate space for counters and restrooms, the *Elizabethton Star* said. In addition, the venue's projection booth was also located in the building.

The Valley Drive-In's amphitheater was completely surfaced and divided by crescent-shaped ramps, which created an unobstructed view for patrons. It also allowed cars entering and leaving the theater to not inconvenience other patrons, and the ramps were designed so that no vehicle would need to back up while in the area, the newspaper reported.

Those visiting the Valley Drive-In entered through a modern two-lane covered box office with a colorfully lighted glass enclosed booth in the center of each lane, the newspaper said. Two cashiers were on duty, and attendants were used to speed up the process.

The Valley Drive-In first opened with a showing of *Law and Order*, a film featuring future U.S. president Ronald Reagan.

In 1964, Hattie Bolling, Earl Bolling's mother, moved to Elizabethton from Norton, Virginia, to help her son with the theater operations. She helped operate the Valley and other theaters. The Bolling family had a seventy-acre farm near Norton, according to the *Elizabethton Star*.

On May 12, 1955, the Valley Drive-In reopened for the summer season with new CinemaScope technology. The owner said the Valley's screen was rebuilt to proportions of ninety-two feet by forty feet for "true CinemaScope," which the newspaper said was viewed without glasses.

The new system at the Valley did not include multiple speakers, but sound was provided via new speakers that could be attached to patrons' vehicles.

The theater closed after a few years and has since become surrounded by residential developments.

Kingsport's Drive-Ins

In 1948, Kingsport welcomed its first drive-in theater. The Bays Mountain Drive-In, which was named in a contest by Mrs. Lee Roy Neal, was located on the Greeneville Highway just outside of the city of Kingsport. It was near the former Pierce Airport, a small local airstrip.

Manager E.W. Algood Jr. operated the theater, according to the *Kingsport Times-News*. The newspaper featured an aerial photograph of the theater, which appears to have sat among the hills. Its single screen could be seen at one end of the amphitheater. There were individual speakers for each car so patrons could enjoy the films.

The Bays Mountain Drive-In is said to have obtained a merchant's license in the summer of 1949. Then, in 1950, a new entrance was built at the drive-in, which featured one movie every day during the week, except for a double feature on Friday and Saturday, according to an advertisement.

"Make this cool, healthful, informal drive-in theater your favorite rendezvous," the advertisement states. "Guard your health by attending your local drive-in movie. Dress as you please, smoke, talk, slip off your shoes. No one will step on your toes. The need for a babysitter is eliminated since parents may tuck their children in the back seat."

The Bays Mountain Drive-In appears to have reopened in 1954 as the 81 Drive-In. A public notice by owner J.R. Pierce said the drive-in had been leased to W.W. Fincher Jr. of Chatsworth, Georgia.

The former Bays Mountain Drive-In, which was located outside of Kingsport, can be seen in this aerial shot of the venue. *City of Kingsport Archives.*

In 1954, the drive-in made newspaper headlines after a robber got away with seventy-five dollars in cash. The *Kingsport Times-News* said a "baby-faced" masked bandit robbed one of the cashiers and demanded all of the money from the cash till. The bandit reportedly said, "Don't do anything foolish. Give me the money or I'll shoot."

The 81 Drive-In appears to have remained open through at least 1958, the last year showings were advertised in the local newspaper.

The Kingsport Drive-In was located along Wilcox Drive, not far from the Eastman Chemical Company. It officially opened on October 27, 1951, and featured the movie *Rogue River*. At the time, the theater was independently operated by Max Wilson.

In 1966, the drive-in became managed by Martin Theatres, which operated several Kingsport venues. That spring, the *Kingsport Times* reported that the drive-in closed for remodeling. When it reopened, the drive-in featured a large new screen, marquee, sound system and concession stand, which operated "cafeteria style." It opened with films featuring Jerry Lewis, Kirk Douglas and Anthony Quinn, the newspaper said.

"We practically built a new drive-in theater," said Lucille Coile, who managed the Martin Theatres' venues.

The Kingsport Drive-In showed its last films on Christmas Eve 1972. It included the double feature *Minnie and Moskowitz* and *Kansas City Bomber*.

At the time, the *Kingsport Times* noted that the theater was located on Eastman Chemical Company property, and the theater's manager told the newspaper that Eastman officials decided they wanted to use the land to increase the amount of parking for employees.

Another Kingsport drive-in operated along four-lane U.S. Highway 11W, which had been known as the New Bristol Highway, from about 1964 to 1985. The Martin Theatres company opened the Marbro Drive-In on November 5, 1964. Although it may have been cold outside, the new theater featured in-car heaters, which allowed the venue to operate throughout the year. It is believed to have been the first in the Tri-Cities to provide in-car heaters for patrons.

With room for 540 cars and a giant screen, it was billed as the largest drive-in theater venue in the area. The Lyle Construction Company, which served as the project's general contractor, said the Marbro was a "credit to our area," according to newspaper articles.

On opening weekend, the theater showed the movies *The 7th Dawn* and *Girls! Girls! Girls!*, starring Elvis Presley.

The Marbro Drive-In served the residents of Kingsport and Sullivan County and was located along U.S. Highway 11W near New Beason Well Road. *City of Kingsport Archives.*

The Marbro remained open until 1985, when it became the last drive-in theater in the Kingsport area to close. The Marbro property remains vacant and is surrounded by residential and commercial developments. Remnants of the former theater's sign can still be seen from the highway.

BRISTOL AND ABINGDON'S DRIVE-INS

The Twin City Drive-In of Bristol, Tennessee, continues to serve the region. It opened along U.S. Highway 11E, or the Volunteer Parkway, on September 26, 1949, and was built by R.A. Warden.

The Warden family continued to operate the venue in the twenty-first century. The theater, with a 350-car capacity, is situated on about twenty-nine acres about six miles from the state line in downtown Bristol and about one mile north of Bristol Motor Speedway, which held its first race more than a decade after the drive-in opened. Beaver Creek Knobs serves as both a boundary and a backdrop to the scenic theater.

Operated by Warden and Bo Diggs, the new venue showcased the Bob Hope film *My Favorite Brunette*.

Warden sold the theater to the aunt and uncle of Danny and Ellen Warden in 1956, according to a written history from the theater. Danny and Ellen Warden then acquired the drive-in theater in 1974.

On October 1, 1977, a dangerous tornado caused extensive damage at the Twin City Drive-In, as well as several other businesses, according to the *Bristol Herald Courier*. The storm damaged the drive-in's original wooden screen tower, which was built from nearby timber.

Within one week, a new Selby Screen Tower was erected, and not a weekend of movies was missed, according to management.

The theater doubles as a temporary campground for the NASCAR and drag races at Bristol Motor Speedway. The theater also includes hot showers and a fire hydrant, which allows the theater to transition into a spot for RVs.

The Beacon Drive-In, another Bristol, Tennessee theater, operated along the Blountville Highway in the mid-twentieth century. It opened on July 3, 1952, and featured James Craig in *Drums in the Deep South*, according to the website CinemaTreasures.org.

Harvey Diggs and T.D. Fields managed the Beacon, which featured in-car heaters.

The Beacon often competed with the Twin City Drive-In, which is located across town, sometimes leading to a price war between the two venues. In 1981, both venues were showing the Clint Eastwood film *Any Which Way You Can*.

At first, the theaters charged regular admission, the *Bristol Herald Courier* said. The Twin City charged $3.00 and the Beacon charged $2.50. By the end of the weekend, however, the Beacon had dropped the price to $1.00.

In order to compete, the Twin City's management dropped the price to fifty cents on the following Monday night. The goal was to "play the game right along with him," the Twin City's manager said.

In response, the Beacon dropped the price to twenty-five cents on Wednesday night.

"I thought, well, if he can undercut me, I'll do my best to undercut him," the Twin City's manager said. So patrons at the Twin City would pay only ten cents per adult to see the movie.

The Beacon made the newspaper's police blotter in 1966. Five of six fugitives who escaped from the Sullivan County jail in Blountville were spotted at the Beacon. They were seen by the manager, who said three men approached him as he was changing the theater's marquee.

Recognizing the fugitives from pictures published in the newspaper, the manager jumped into his car and drove to the theater box to call authorities,

the *Bristol Herald Courier* said. Only minutes before, the manager's wife said she was accosted by the escapees while taking her parents to their home near the theater.

Police went to the theater and had a police dog track them into the woods, but they were not located.

The Beacon closed in 1983, which is the last year the venue advertised showings in the newspaper. By 1984, ten acres of prime property at the Beacon site was available for sale for $100,000. Today, a Dollar General store and an apartment complex are located at the site of the former Beacon Drive-In.

Another drive-in theater, the Moonlite, operated along Lee Highway, or U.S. Highway 11, near Abingdon, Virginia. It opened during the summer of

The Beacon Drive-In, currently the site of a Dollar General store and apartment complex, was just outside of the city of Bristol, Tennessee. *City of Kingsport Archives.*

1949 and quickly became a highly successful operation under the ownership of T.D. Fields, who also managed the Beacon. It had a capacity of 454 cars.

Patrons took advantage of the low admission prices and reasonably priced hot dogs, sodas and other concessions, according to the Moonlite's National Register of Historic Places nomination form.

During the 1950s and 1960s, the Moonlite became a local institution and a mainstay of weekend evening entertainment and recreation in Southwest Virginia. Business at the Moonlite began to wane in the 1960s and 1970s.

The Moonlite Drive-In is one of a handful of drive-ins listed on the National Register of Historic Places in the United States. *Author photo.*

In 1964, Fields sold the theater to Walter Mays, who in turn later sold it to William Booker in 1992. The Moonlite closed in 2013 but later reopened in 2016. The theater stayed open for a short amount of time and closed again.

In 2020, the Moonlite briefly opened when the Barter Theatre began performing on a stage at the drive-in during the COVID-19 pandemic. Thousands of patrons could sit safely in their vehicles, listen to the show on the radio and either watch the stage or watch the show on the big screen.

On March 29, 2024, the Moonlite was sold to the Blevins and Crusenberry families of Abingdon. The Moonline was expected to open in 2025.

DRIVE-INS OF THE ENVIRONS

The environs of the Tri-Cities were home to numerous drive-in theaters during the twentieth century.

The town of Erwin was home to the Holiday Drive-In. In 1952, Earle Hendren, president of Capitol Amusements, announced that a new five-hundred-car-capacity drive-in would be constructed just outside of the town. His company also owned the town's Lyric and Capitol theaters.

The Holiday Drive-In sat on eight acres and was located near Ohio Avenue and Mohawk Drive. The new drive-in opened the same month that the Lyric Theatre closed, according to the *Erwin Record*.

A new CinemaScope screen was installed at the Holiday Drive-In on April 5, 1956. The theater appears to have finally closed in the 1980s.

Three drive-in theaters—the Nite Auto Movie, Ashway Drive-In and Woodside Drive-In—once operated in or near the town of Greeneville, Tennessee.

The *Greeneville Sun* said Ernest W. Knight and his wife opened the Nite Auto Movie theater in 1949. It was located on about six acres of land along Tusculum Boulevard at a site that later became the Greeneville Commons shopping center.

It was complete with modern restrooms and a refreshment counter in the centrally located projection house. Patrons could enjoy soft drinks, popcorn, ice cream and sandwiches from the refreshment center.

"An exclusive feature of the drive-in theater is that popcorn may be eaten in the privacy of your car without disturbing the neighboring patrons," the *Greeneville Sun* said.

The theater could originally serve 250 cars. The venue's first nine ramps were designated for cars while the tenth ramp was reserved for trucks, the newspaper said.

Patrons could also enjoy a hayride, and parties were permitted with advanced reservations. The plan was to show three films during the week, but they would change every Monday, Wednesday and Friday. In addition, the drive-in showcased both feature films and shorts.

The films were shown on a giant screen tower that measured forty-five feet high by forty-nine feet wide. It featured the latest sound equipment, and portable speakers could be attached to the inside of each car.

By 1955, the theater was owned by W.J. Hatfield, according to CinemaTreasures.org.

In January 1960, the Nite Auto Movie's concession stand was gutted by fire, according to the *Greeneville Sun*. The fire was believed to have started from a fryer, which may have been left on, the fire chief told the newspaper.

The theater reopened in February, but by March, the theater had been sold to E.L. Wilson, the newspaper said. Wilson also opened the Ashway Drive-In. He planned to rebuild the Nite Auto's concession stand and said he would show only movies that were suitable for the entire family.

The exact closing date of the Nite Auto is unknown, but the last advertisement for the theater appears to have been published in late 1961.

The Ashway Drive-In appears to have opened in 1951, just west of Greeneville, on the Asheville Highway. It was later remodeled and celebrated a grant reopening in the spring of 1954 with a showing of Charlton Heston's *Pony Express*, according to the *Greeneville Sun*. The drive-in featured what was described at the time as "Tennessee's widest outdoor movie screen" at sixty-nine feet long by thirty-nine feet wide.

In addition, the Ashway featured a playground complete with swings and slides, as well as a patio for those who wanted to watch movies under the moonlight. A new modern concession stand and restrooms were also provided.

Work on the remodeled Ashway began in late 1953, and the newspaper said some forty-three thousand yards of dirt were evacuated from the site to give a more gradual slope. Ultimately, the drive-in had a four-hundred-car capacity, the newspaper reported.

The Ashway Drive-In last advertised in the *Greeneville Sun* at the end of 1963, wishing the public a Merry Christmas.

In 1954, the *Greeneville Sun* reported that the Woodside Drive-In Theatre would open along Snapps Ferry Road, near Anderson's Super Market and the Magnavox No. 2 plant, a large electronics manufacturer. Greeneville businessman Bob Craft and his wife owned and operated the new drive-in, the newspaper said. Craft also owned the Home Bedding Company in Greeneville. His wife served as the drive-in's cashier.

The new drive-in had a capacity of two hundred cars and "is another step in the fast-moving progress of Greeneville," the newspaper said. With a thirty-five-by-fifty-five-foot screen, the Woodside opened with *The Wild North*, which starred Stewart Granger and Cyd Charisse.

Craft's wife told the newspaper that the theater would go back and pick up "the cream of the crop" of older films that had been requested by the public.

The Woodside Drive-In stayed open through 1956. It transitioned into the Woodlawn Grill in late 1957.

The Hi-Land Drive-In opened in early October 1950, just outside of the town of Rogersville in Hawkins County, Tennessee. It was located about two and a half miles east of town near U.S. Highway 11W.

"I am using this medium to express my thanks to every person and firm that in any way worked on and cooperated in the building and opening of the Hi-Land Drive-In Theatre, Rogersville's new amusement center," the theater's owner said in an advertisement following the grand opening.

The advertisement, which was published in the *Rogersville Review* newspaper, said the venue's speakers would begin playing music every night at 6:30 p.m.

One film would begin playing at 7:00 p.m., and after a short intermission, another show would start around 9:00 p.m.

About two hundred cars could fit into the lot at the Hi-Land Drive-In.

Another drive-in, the Jolly Roger, opened in 1962 on Stanley Valley Road near Rogersville. The three-hundred-car-capacity drive-in featured a 150-by-55-foot CinemaScope screen, a modern snack bar and clean restrooms, the new theater advertised in the *Rogersville Review*.

Owned and operated by E.L. Wilson, who also operated drive-in theaters in Greeneville, the Jolly Roger opened with the film *Second Time Around*.

Both the Hi-Land and the Jolly Roger closed sometime in the mid-1960s, the last time both drive-in theaters were advertised in the *Rogersville Review*.

A drive-in theater briefly operated in 2021 on Choptack Road, just west of Rogersville. A couple had moved from Alaska to a one-hundred-acre farm and decided to open a new fundraiser drive-in theater, according to an article in the newspaper.

Proceeds from the venue, which featured a forty-foot drive-in theater screen, benefited local schools. Holston Electric Cooperative and WRGS Radio assisted the operation. The costs of operating a drive-in became too much, and the operation closed at the end of the season.

In rural Johnson County, Tennessee, just outside of Mountain City, a drive-in theater opened in the 1950s. It was located on U.S. Highway 421, just outside of town.

The Mountaineer Drive-In held about 175 to 200 cars, depending on who was counting. It was operated by W.B. Hamaker, according to the *Tomahawk* newspaper.

The Sundown Theatre, located at the river bridge along U.S. Highway 23, in Weber City, Virginia, opened in the late 1940s. It apparently had been remodeled and reopened on April 1, 1949, according to an article in the *Kingsport Times*.

In 1949, the manager, Reginald Fuller, said the theater's field had been enlarged and could accommodate about twice the number of cars as the previous year. It was also completely redesigned and terraced to give every patron a clear view of the screen.

The theater's main entrance was novel for a drive-in theater, the newspaper said. The entrance building featured the administrative offices, the ticket office and concessions. To enter the lot, patrons would drive under the building's roof, the newspaper said.

Fuller said a treat was in store for the drive-in's patrons because each night the field would be lighted up by the moon.

"This was accomplished at a great amount of expense to be of service to all patrons," the newspaper said. "This certainly makes an ideal setting on the banks of the Holston River."

The Sundown added in-car speakers in 1952 and apparently operated until 1961. After it closed, the site was used for flea markets.

Weber City gained a second drive-in theater in the summer of 1953. The owners of the Taylor Drive-In claimed to operate the largest and most modern drive-in in the area. It featured 450 car spaces, each with individual speakers, and the entire area was more than ten acres, according to the *Kingsport Times*.

The Taylor family, which also operated theaters in nearby Kingsport, installed a sixty-five-by-fifty-six-foot screen at the drive-in. The venue's concession stand could reportedly serve 420 people every fifteen minutes and featured short orders, ice cream and cold drinks.

The opening attraction was *Fair Wind to Java*, which starred Fred MacMurray and Vera Ralston.

In 1971, local authorities raided the Taylor Drive-In. It resulted in the arrest of the manager and the seizure of the film being shown that night on February 18, Kingsport newspapers reported. The Town of Weber City and the theater's owner, Martin Theatres, had apparently disagreed for some time over the types of movies being shown at the venue.

The venue had been showing X-rated films and allowed minors to view them, authorities said. One night, the police chief and town mayor went to the theater and went from car to car to check the ages of the occupants. Several children were present, authorities said.

While charges were being filed, the sheriff's office received a report that rotten eggs were being thrown at the Weber City mayor's house.

"I hope you catch whoever's doing that," the theater's operator said. "He's no friend of the theater."

One of the patrons who attended the movie told the newspaper afterward that "the raid was more exciting than the show."

The Taylor Drive-In closed in 1976. The site is now home to a Food City supermarket.

The towns of Glade Spring and Damascus in Washington County, Virginia, each had one drive-in theater. The Summit Drive-In opened in 1953 near Glade Spring along Virginia State Route 91. It was operated by Joseph L. Meek, who also ran the drive-in theater in nearby Damascus.

The Laurel Drive-In also opened about 1953 and was located on Route 91 near U.S. Highway 58 in Damascus. Both the Summit and Laurel showcased X-rated films in the 1970s until they closed in the mid-1980s. Advertisements in the *Bristol Herald Courier* for the theaters showed images of scantily clad women.

The screen tower at the Summit was eventually removed from the site in 1998. Its giant marquee later was relocated to a storage lot along Lee Highway, or U.S. Highway 11, near Abingdon. The Summit's sign, as well as a sign for the legendary Robert E. Lee Motel, can be seen by passersby.

Two drive-in theaters operated from the 1950s to the 1980s in Russell County, Virginia, according to CinemaTreasures.org. The Bluegrass was located in Castlewood near the Russell County Fairgrounds and the Cavalier was in Lebanon along U.S. Highway 19. The Cavalier was heavily damaged by floodwaters in 1957, according to the *Bristol Herald Courier*.

Remnants of the Lonesome Pine Drive-In can still be seen along U.S. Highway 58 in Coeburn, Virginia. It opened in 1946 and closed sometime in the 1990s. Its sign, some of the vehicle ramps and a screen can still be seen along the highway.

A few drive-in theaters once operated in Wise County. The Hi-Way Drive-In opened on Virginia State Route 70 and was operated by Earl Mullins, who managed several local theaters. Another drive-in theater opened between Big Stone Gap and Norton in 1952. The Powell Valley Drive-In Theatre also hosted an Independence Day fireworks celebration, according to the *Big Stone Gap Post*.

In 1979, the Viking Drive-In opened. It was named in honor of the local Powell Valley High School Vikings athletics program. It remained open for about a year.

The Mullins Open Air Theater opened in the center of the town of Wise in 1946. Located in the 200 block of Railroad Avenue Northeast, the theater's name changed to the Wise Drive-In by the mid-1950s. It closed a few years later and transitioned into a shopping center.

The Central Drive-In of Wise County remained open in 2024. It is located on Kent Junction Road in 1952 in the Blackwood community, just outside of Norton. The Kiser family originally opened the venue and operated it for decades until Buddy and Paula Herron purchased the venue in 2005.

The town of Marion, Virginia, has been home to two drive-in theaters, the Skyview and Park Place, which originally opened in 1954 and was open as of this writing. The Skyview was at the corner of U.S. Highway 11 and Adwolfe Road and opened in 1949. It was later demolished for the construction of Interstate 81 but was relocated and reopened. It finally closed in 1988 and transitioned into the Skyview Equipment Company.

8

MODERN MOVIE HOUSES

During the mid- to late twentieth century, suburban malls in America became host to a variety of businesses, including department stores, restaurants, amusement attractions and movie theaters.

Before malls opened in the 1960s and 1970s, most suburban residents would shop, eat and watch movies in downtown areas or head to the smaller nearby towns to visit mom-and-pop businesses. Developers believed malls would provide a closer and more modern alternative for those who did not live near downtown.

THE MIRACLE MALL

In the 1970s, developers began to build and open enclosed shopping malls in the Tri-Cities. The Miracle Mall was the region's first. It was constructed in northern Johnson City or about three miles from the city's downtown district.

With twenty businesses, including a Sears department store, the Miracle Mall opened on March 17, 1971, along North Roan Street. The single-screen Mall Theatre opened three months later and featured Ryan O'Neal in *Love Story*. It was first operated by ABC Southeastern Theatre Inc., and the company's president, J.H. Harrison, attended the grand opening ceremonies.

The new theater featured a screen that curved into the wall, according to advertisements. The lens used in the projectors were designed to match the curve of the screen and project and evenly distribute the image. It accommodated 625 patrons.

The Johnson City theater was twinned in 1979 and by 1990 was operated by Plitt Theatres as the Mall 1 and 2 Theatres. The theater eventually closed in 1993. The final movies screened were Chevy Chase in *Fletch Lives* and Kevin Bernhardt in *Hellraiser III: Hell on Earth*.

The movie theater at the facility, which is now known as the Mall of Johnson City, was demolished shortly after its closing.

BRISTOL MALL

A movie theater opened on May 7, 1976, at the Bristol Mall along Gate City Highway in Bristol, Virginia. The mall was located about two and a half miles from downtown Bristol. The theater venue was operated by American Multi-Cinema, a nationally recognized theater operator known as AMC Theatres.

Located on the mall's lower level, the theater featured four separate soundproof auditoriums. The auditoriums were clustered around a common box office, lobby and concession area.

"The concept of the multi-film theater complex is that of reaching the entire family," Jeff Schnabel, field operator for AMC, told the *Bristol Herald Courier*. "We want the entire family to come to the theater and have an opportunity to select a film that would appeal to all ages within the family."

Virginia's first casino opened in 2022 at the site of the former Bristol Mall, which was home to a four-screen movie theater. Construction of the casino continued in 2024. *Author photo.*

The Bristol Mall's theater was the first such multi-auditorium complex within a wide radius at the time of its opening in 1976, according to the newspaper.

"We believe the people in this area will respond to the multi-film concept as others across the country have," Schnabel told the newspaper. "This concept seems to be the answer to modern movie going, giving people a choice to make from several films all under one roof."

Two additional screens were added in 1981. Then, in 1991, Carmike Theatres took over operations of the venue.

Like many malls around the country in the twenty-first century, the Bristol Mall began to see fewer visitors. The approximately 550,000-square-foot mall also began to lose business.

In 2008, the *Bristol Herald Courier* reported that the mall venue had closed. Rows of posters promoting out-of-date movies had littered the floor outside the locked doors of the darkened Village Theatres, which the venue had been named at the time, the newspaper said.

Village Entertainment, a Chicago, Illinois–based firm, had renovated and reopened the theater in 2005. The company still had multiple years remaining on its lease, mall management told the newspaper in 2008.

The theater then reopened a short time later by Visionary Theaters, another Chicago firm. Business continued to dwindle at the mall, and the theater finally shuttered in 2015.

The Bristol Mall finally closed in late 2017, when the final business, KSS School Supplies, moved. The mall is not alone. The number of malls in the United States fell from 1,500 in 2005 to about 1,150 by late 2022, according to the International Council of Shopping Centers.

After the mall closed, a pharmaceutical company converted the vacant property into a cannabidiol production plant. But in 2021, local officials announced plans to transform the former mall site into the Hard Rock Hotel & Casino Bristol. A temporary casino opened in July 2022 while crews worked on the larger permanent resort casino.

FORT HENRY MALL

The Fort Henry Mall, which included three department stores and a five-screen movie theater, opened in 1976 in Kingsport. AMC, which also operated the Bristol theater, opened the Fort Henry movie house on August 27, 1976. Additional screens were later added.

Fort Henry Mall transitioned into the Kingsport Town Center in 2007 after a California company purchased the property. Significant plans were made to renovate and expand the mall, including in the theater area, but those did not come to fruition.

In 2013, the theater, which had been operated by Marquee Cinemas for more than a decade, reopened as Frank Theatres. The new operator opened only ten of the property's eleven auditoriums and had plans for future expansion.

Later, in 2017, the theater was taken over by NCG Cinemas, or Neighborhood Cinema Group. That year, under the ownership of the Hull Property Group, the Kingsport Town Center once again became the Fort Henry Mall.

In 2023, the IMAX Corporation and NCG Cinemas announced a plan to open an IMAX theater at the Fort Henry Mall. IMAX is a process of film projection using a giant screen on which an image approximately ten times larger than standard is projected. Such theaters are typically larger and taller than normal movie houses, according to IMAX.

Once it opens, the new theater will be the only IMAX venue in the Tri-Cities region. In 2024, the closest IMAX was at the Regal Pinnacle just west of Knoxville, Tennessee.

THE FORGOTTEN MALL

The Martin Theatre, a movie house that once anchored the former Kingsport Mall, operated for a few decades on Eastman Road. The new single-screen theater opened to the public on June 24, 1971, and was managed by Lucille Coile, who had also directed the Strand Theatre, Marbro Drive-In, Kingsport Drive-In and the Taylor Drive-In Theatre. The venue opened with John Wayne in *Big Jake*.

"We'll try to show one for general audiences and adult audiences at the same time at the Martin and the Strand so everyone can find a movie to see that week," Coile told the *Kingsport Times-News*.

The Martin was located between the Hills and Montgomery Ward department stores at the new Kingsport Mall on Eastman Road, not far from its intersection with East Stone Drive. Patrons could access the theater from either the front or back of the mall complex.

Visitors wanting to know what was playing could either check the local newspaper or view "next attractions" displays at the theater's entrance. The signs featured bubble lights to make them stand out to patrons.

"One thing we're especially proud of is the rocking chair seats," Coile said. "You can lean back as far as you like without disturbing the person in the row behind you."

The theater had a total seating capacity of 550 people. By 1982, the venue had been converted into a twin cinema and became known as the Martin Twin.

In 1988, the Martin became a "sub-run" theater, which means it began to show movies after they had already been shown at first-run venues in the city. At the time, it was operated by Carmike Theatres. The theater chain sought to compete with other theaters, and tickets cost $1.50 a person for a showing.

The Martin was believed to have been the second movie house in Carmike's southeast region, following one in Asheville, North Carolina, that became a sub-run theater. The newspaper said attendance at the Kingsport venue went up 30 percent following the change.

It appears that the Martin closed in the early 1990s. In addition, the mall, which also featured a Giant Food market, White Cross Drugs and Scott's variety store, gradually closed. The final department store, Montgomery Ward, closed in 2000.

In 2024, few remnants of the mall remained. Office Depot is the only remaining store from the former mall. The site has since transitioned into the East Stone Commons.

Multiplex Theaters

In addition to mall movie theaters, other venues were established away from the downtown districts of the Tri-Cities region, including one that opened in 1974 on Volunteer Parkway in Bristol, Tennessee. Tom Curtin's Holiday Cinema operated at the Plaza Shopping Center

The theater had seats for 300 people and was in the space formerly occupied by a dry-cleaning plant and a beauty shop. Its smaller auditorium followed the trend of modern theater construction, according to the *Bristol Herald Courier*. In 1972, a total of 502 theaters were constructed in the United States, and almost 60 percent of those theaters had auditoriums seating 350 people or less, the newspaper said.

The Holiday Cinema was the city's first theater to feature fully automated projection and sound equipment. The older theaters in downtown Bristol along State Street had full-time projectionists who handled the equipment. The theater was also the first modern theater to open outside of downtown Bristol, where the Cameo and Paramount theaters still operated.

The new venue had plenty of free parking and new plush seats, according to a newspaper advertisement. Curtin, the Holiday's owner, was also a juggler and performed nightly at clubs in the area. Both professions were reflected in Curtin's childhood fascinations. He was a movie fan who grew up laughing at the antics of Laurel and Hardy, and he was a fan of Charlie Chaplin, Harold Lloyd and the Marx Brothers, according to the *Bristol Herald Courier*. He is also a past president of the International Jugglers Association.

The juggler's Holiday Cinema had added a second screen by the early 1980s, but the venue eventually closed in about 1988. The theater's site continues to serve as a shopping center.

Tinseltown Bristol, a modern megaplex near Interstate 81, opened on November 13. 1998. The Cinemark theater was lured to Bristol, Virginia, by C&J Associates, a development firm owned by local businessmen Tim Carter and Steve Johnson, according to the *Bristol Herald Courier*.

"We want to thank Cinemark for bringing us one of the largest movie theaters in Southwest Virginia and Upper East Tennessee," former city councilman Doug Weberling said at the opening, which had about three thousand invitees.

City officials said they hoped Tinseltown would draw other businesses to the mostly undeveloped Bristol Commons complex off Interstate 81. The Holiday Inn Convention Center and an O'Charley's restaurant were nearby.

Tinseltown was expected to draw about 700,000 theatergoers a year and generate more than $200,000 annually in taxes, according to an early proposal.

The theater remained a popular venue for years, gathering residents from around the region to Bristol. Its run ended in early May 2020, during the height of the COVID-19 pandemic. Like other venues around the country, the pandemic led theaters to close their doors.

"Cinemark can confirm that its Tinseltown 14 theater in Bristol, Virginia, will not reopen as it is nearing the conclusion of its lease term," the company told the *Bristol Herald Courier*. "This closure is normal course of business and the result of the careful and ongoing review of our theater fleet."

After the closing, officials attracted the attention of Legacy Theaters, which had previously reopened a closed theater in the Staunton, Virginia area. Legacy Theaters reopened the Bristol movie house in September 2020. In 2024, Legacy operated theaters in Bristol and Flowood, Mississippi. It serves as a second-run movie theater.

Another movie megaplex opened in Bristol, Tennessee, at the Pinnacle, a 240-acre mixed-use complex, on November 19, 2015. The new Pinnacle 12 Marquee Cinemas cost about $12 million and featured state-of-the-art equipment. The fifty-five-thousand-square-foot theater offered Dolby sound, online ticketing, digital projection and reserved seating, Marquee officials told the media prior to its opening. The entire theater also had 1,454 electric luxury recliners.

"The difference between having luxury recliners and regular seating is like flying coach or first class," said James Cox, chief operating officer for Marquee Cinemas.

Johnson, the local developer, said the Marquee theater offered a fantastic amenity for the region. "I don't know of another complex like this within a hundred miles," Johnson told the *Bristol Herald Courier*. "This is better than an IMAX; it's certainly the cherry on top of what we've done to date."

The first movies to be shown at the Marquee included the blockbusters *The Martian* and *The Hunger Games: Mockingjay Part 2*.

A movie megaplex operated for about two decades in a now defunct outlet mall in Blountville, Tennessee. The Tri-Cities 7 Cinema opened in the Factory Stores of America complex near Interstate 81 on April 16, 1999. The outlet center, which also included a popular Carolina Pottery store, was established in 1990.

The seven-screen theater featured "stealth cinema," a new technology that uses curved screens set at forty-five-degree angles to the audience. Its auditoriums also featured new stadium-style seating.

In 2009, the theater reopened under new management. The owner, Paul Wylie, owned several theaters in Johnson City and Knoxville.

The Tri-Cities 7 Cinema was forced to close in 2020 due to the COVID-19 pandemic. Management reopened the theater a couple months later, but it was then permanently closed in 2021. A manager told local media that online streaming services hurt the theater industry and Tri-Cities 7 Cinema was unable to bounce back following the pandemic.

In late 2020, it was announced that Larkspur, a real estate development company, had acquired the shopping center. The company had plans to redevelop the 23.26-acre site. A storage company currently occupies a portion of the site.

Johnson City has been home to a few suburban-type multiplexes, including the Parkway Cinema and the Real to Reel Theaters. The Parkway officially opened on January 28, 1971, and featured a showing of *Goodbye, Mr. Chips* with Peter O'Toole. Planning for the new theater began in 1970, and several houses and mobile homes were moved from the site in north Johnson City.

The theater was the primary unit of a business complex built by Jim Kalogeros, a Johnson City restaurateur. It was leased and operated by

The Tri-Cities 7 Cinema in Blountville, Tennessee, was one of the victims of the COVID-19 pandemic. It closed in 2021. *Author photo.*

Appalachian Enterprises. E.R. Miller, president of Appalachian Enterprises, spoke to the *Johnson City Press* in 1970 about the new theater.

"It will include the latest ultra-modern projection equipment and approximately 530 rocking chair type seats, spaced 40 inches apart for added comfort," Miller said. "The building will be air conditioned and will have a snack bar."

Local Johnson City architect Hugh H. Gaddis designed the single-story brick structure. Located across from the mall, which opened in 1971, the Parkway featured a box office in the foyer and about twenty-five thousand square feet of floor space.

In 1972, Appalachian Enterprises sold the Capri and the Parkway to local theater operator Paul Wylie. The Parkway Cinema eventually added a second screen and reopened as a twin theater. It closed in 1983 with a showing of Anthony Perkins in *Psycho II*.

After it closed, the Parkway reopened as the United Clothing Store. Since then, several other businesses have occupied the former Parkway's space, including restaurants, nightclubs and bars.

The same year that Wylie closed the Parkway, he also opened the Real to Reel Theaters, a four-auditorium movie house. The Real to Real was named by a local resident who submitted one of 1,200 entries for a contest to name the new theater.

The theater, designed by architect Ken Ross, could seat about one thousand people and was equipped with fully automated projectors, one of which was outfitted with the capability to run three-dimensional films. Cartoon characters of prominent Johnson Citians decorated the interior, according to the *Johnson City Press*.

The Real to Reel was originally a first-run theater and showed some of the biggest blockbusters but eventually transitioned into a second-run or sub-run theater. It would show movies that had already been shown elsewhere and had discount prices.

A few months after opening the theater, Wylie sold the Real to Reel to a Knoxville theater operator. Like other theaters around the country, the Real to Reel closed in March 2020 due to the COVID-19 pandemic. A few months later, in July 2020, it was announced that the theater would not reopen. Peerless Properties and Development, which operated a popular restaurant near the theater, said the property would be redeveloped.

The city of Johnson City's most modern movie house to date originally opened on October 24, 1986, and continues to operate in the twenty-first century. Johnson City's Cinema AMC opened with eight screens near the mall. At the time, operations manager Phil Pennington said the theater would seat about 1,600 people. AMC, which in 2024 was the largest theater company in the country, also opened theaters in the 1970s at the malls in Kingsport and Bristol.

In 1991, the AMC theaters in Johnson City, Bristol and Kingsport were sold to Carmike Theaters, but managers told patrons that they would likely not notice any difference in films or prices. At that time, the venue's name changed to Johnson City 8 Theaters.

Eight years later, in 1999, Carmike announced that it was closing the theater's doors and turning off the projectors for about eight months for a reconstruction. Crews then began to demolish the theater and construct a new venue with stadium seating and a digital sound system.

"We will be closing the doors to do a retrofit and an add on," Carmike's assistant vice president told the *Johnson City Press* in 1999. "It is going to be demolished and rebuilt with 100 percent stadium seating and 100 percent digital sound. It should reopen in May."

At about the same time that the Carmike closed, a Murfreesboro, Tennessee developer said Oregon-based Wallace Theaters was planning to open a fourteen-screen cineplex near the corner of Knob Creek Road and State of Frankling Road. By 2000, however, that project was on hold, and it was eventually canceled.

After some delay, the new Carmike theater reopened in November 2020. It opened with high ceilings and two concessions, as well as fourteen screens and state-of-the-art equipment. The AMC Johnson City 14 remained open in 2024 off North Roan Street.

A movie megaplex operated for about two decades in a now defunct-outlet mall in Blountville, Tennessee.

The Tri-Cities 7 Cinema opened in the Factory Stores of America complex near Interstate 81 on April 16, 1999. The outlet center, which also included a popular Carolina Pottery store, had been established in 1990.

The seven-screen theater was developed by ShoPro Inc. and featured new stealth cinema technology. The new technique featured curved screens set at forty-five-degree angles to the audience in a theater auditorium. It also featured new stadium-style seating.

In 2009, the theater reopened under new management. The owner, Paul Wylie, owned several theaters in Johnson City and Knoxville.

The Tri-Cities 7 Cinema was forced to close in 2020 due to the COVID-19 pandemic. Management reopened the theater a couple months later, but it was then permanently closed in 2021.

A manager told local media that online streaming services hurt the theater industry and Tri-Cities 7 Cinema was unable to bounce back following the pandemic. Before the pandemic, the manager told WCYB-TV that the theater would see more than one thousand people on a weekend. Shortly before it closed, the theater had only about fifty people.

In late 2020, it was announced that Larkspur, a real estate development company, had acquired the shopping center. The company plans to redevelop the 23.26-acre site. A storage company currently occupies a portion of the site. Other businesses, including the theater and Carolina Pottery, are closed.

A movie house known as the Terrace Theatre once operated in a now defunct shopping plaza along West Stone Drive in Kingsport.

Ground was broken in the spring of 1970 at the future site of the twenty-acre Kings-Giant Plaza on Stone Drive near its intersection with Clinchfield Street and Bloomingdale Road. The original plans called for twenty retail and service stores surrounded by a huge parking lot designed to accommodate 1,200 cars. The center was designed to include extra-wide covered sidewalks for all-weather shopping and brick storefronts, according to an article about the project in the *Kingsport News*.

Stores to open at the new shopping center included Tennessee's first King's Department Store, Giant Food Market, Gateway Book Store, White Cross pharmacy, a branch of the First National Bank of Sullivan County and a new movie theater. The 137,000-square-foot center was developed by Independent Enterprises of Chattanooga, Tennessee.

The ABC Southeastern Theatre company, also known as the American Broadcasting Corporation, opened the Terrace Theatre at the development on April 1, 1971, approximately one year after groundbreaking. Its opening featured Kurt Russell in *The Barefoot Executive*.

Eddie Taylor served as the new theater's house manager. Eight employees, including ushers, ticket sellers and concession workers, worked under his leadership, according to the *Kingsport News*. ABC also operated the Paramount Theatre in Bristol, where Taylor worked before going to the Terrace.

The ABC company also had a managing director, Donald Kent, who led both the Terrace Theatre and the State Theatre in downtown Kingsport. The two theaters would show entirely different films each week, and it was policy that neither venue would show an X-rated film.

"When families want to go out to a movie, it's hard to find one that's good entertainment for the whole group," Kent said. "By having more theaters in Kingsport we'll be able to show different types of films to please more people."

A second screen was added to the Terrace in late 1979. In 1990, the theater was sold by Cineplex Odeon Theatres to Carmike Cinemas, according to an article in the *Kingsport Times*.

Many Kingsport residents recall seeing *Jaws* and *Home Alone* at the Terrace. The theater and other businesses at the shopping center closed in the 1990s.

In 1999, Wellmont Health System received state approval to convert the former Kings-Giant Plaza into a seventy-thousand-square-foot outpatient imaging and rehabilitation center and a six-room ambulatory surgery center.

The site of the former Terrace Theatre and the shopping plaza is now covered with parking lots and medical facilities.

The town of Greeneville has been home to two suburban movie houses, the Capri Theatre and the AMC Classic Towne Crossing 8, both of which operated along the U.S. Highway 11E Bypass.

The Capri originally opened with one screen and was in operation by the 1970s. Eventually, Carmike Theatres, a movie theater chain headquartered in Columbus, Georgia, updated the theater and converted the Capri into a twin theater.

A *Greeneville Sun* story says the Capri ultimately closed in late 2008. By that time, the Capri had become a discount second-run theater and lost a considerable amount of business to a more modern and larger megaplex farther west on "the bypass."

Phoenix Theatres opened an eight-screen megaplex in Greeneville on February 22, 2006. It was estimated to cost about $5 million and was designed by the RLS Design Group. The theater featured multiple auditoriums, including two with 270 seats, two with 159 seats, two with 145 seats and two with 97 seats, according to CinemaTreasures.org.

Carmike Theatres later purchased the megaplex and added digital and three-dimensional state-of-the-art equipment. In 2017, the theater became the AMC Classic Towne Crossing 8 after AMC acquired Carmike Cinemas in a $1.1 billion deal. The theater temporarily closed during the COVID-19 pandemic in 2020 but remained opened in 2024.

The Abingdon Cinemall, an independent theater, opened in February 1998 in the 700 block of East Main Street. When it opened, Abingdon had no movie theater, and it was theorized that the town's population would not be able to support a new venue, according to an advertisement in the *Bristol Herald Courier* newspaper.

In 1998, however, Steve Weston opened the Abingdon Cinemall at the east end of town. After opening, the venue added a laser tag arena and an interactive shooting gallery. Public support of the Cinemall was so strong that the theater added a restaurant and other activities over the years.

The Abingdon theater, which had stadium-style seating, ran mainstream first-run motion pictures and art films. The film *Titanic*, which received eleven Academy Awards, was especially popular at the new Cinemall and remained on the schedule for several months.

During its history, the Cinemall was showcased on ABC's *Good Morning America* in 1999 as one of the top three theaters in the country to show *Star Wars*. The theater has seated patrons from forty-two different states and nine foreign countries, according to the owner.

In 2014, the Abingdon Cinemall was one of about three hundred theaters, including the only one in the Tri-Cities region, to showcase *The Interview*, a controversial film from Sony Pictures that drew condemnation from North Korea.

"We're not going to be censored by anybody," Weston told media outlets. "That's not going to happen in Southwest Virginia."

Weston's theater has shown a variety of films over the years, including major blockbusters and small independent films. The theater remained open in 2024.

9

SPECIALTY THEATERS

THE CARTER FAMILY FOLD

The Carter Family Fold, a rustic venue dedicated to the "First Family of Country Music," is located in the community of Hiltons in rural Scott County, Virginia. The venue, which hosts musical performances every Saturday night from February to November, celebrated its fiftieth anniversary in 2024.

Rita Forrester, who manages the Carter Family Fold, spoke to Marina Waters, a Six Rivers Media journalist, in 2023 about the work that went into the venue, which her family built in 1976.

"I saw the store renovated, the Fold built, we moved the cabin, I was hands-on for every bit of that," Forrester said.

Forrester was referring to her grandfather's childhood cabin that now sits on the property along A.P. Carter Highway, as well as the old store where Carter Fold performances were first held.

Janette Carter, the daughter of Alvin Pleasant "A.P." Carter of the legendary Carter Family, founded the venue in the 1970s. Today, the Carter Family Memorial Music Center is a nonprofit organization serving fans and supporters of old-time country and folk music. It is directed by Janette Carter's daughter Forrester.

A.P. Carter grew up in the isolated mountain community of Maces Spring, according to the National Register of Historic Places, which includes buildings connected with the Carter family. In his early years, A.P. became interested in music and sang in the church choir and in a family quartet, and he also learned to play the fiddle.

In June 1915, A.P. married Sara Dougherty, who was also musically inclined and played several instruments. The third member of the Carter Family, Maybelle Addington, Sara's cousin, married A.P.'s brother in 1926 and moved to Maces Spring.

The group's first major break occurred in the summer of 1927, when the Victor Talking Machine Company auditioned local talent in nearby Bristol, Tennessee. They performed a wide repertoire of traditional songs, including old ballads, occupational songs, hymns and gospel music, Victorian parlor songs and other sentimental pieces and Black-inspired blues songs collected from throughout the region.

The Carter Family ultimately performed about 250 songs between 1927 and the 1940s, preserving a valuable part of Appalachian history.

Over the years, the family disbanded, and each member went his or her own way. "Mother" Maybelle went on to perform with her daughters, which included June Carter, who became a successful solo performer. June Carter married country singer Johnny Cash. A.P. Carter, who died in 1960, and Sara Carter, who died in 1971, became less involved in the public sphere. Maybelle Carter died in 1978.

A.P. built his general store in the heart of Maces Spring in 1945 but still had intentions of remaining active in music, according to the national register. His daughter Janette Carter later used the store for traditional music shows.

The rustic Carter Family Fold was built in 1976 and featured more than eight hundred seats. It hosts live music performances. In addition to the stage and seating area, the Fold includes a large dance floor, where visitors and performers can enjoy traditional Appalachian dances like clogging.

Johnny Cash, who married into the Carter family and is known for his hit songs "I Walk the Line" and "Ring of Fire," performed at the Fold several times over the years and played his last public concert there a few months before he died in 2023.

Guests of the Fold can also visit the relocated and restored 1880s cabin and birthplace of A.P. Carter, as well as the nearby Carter museum, both of which are on the National Register of Historic Places.

COUNTRY CABIN

The Country Cabin is a historic music venue in Wise County and the longest continuously running venue for traditional music along the Crooked Road, which showcases old-time music in Southwest Virginia.

The venue's history started back in 1937 as a small gathering of bluegrass and country pickers, according to the *Bristol Herald Courier*. The Country Cabin, a simple log structure, was built around 1937 with the encouragement of local ballad singer and songwriter Kate O'Neill Peters Sturgill, according to the Crooked Road, which includes the venue.

The popularity of the weekly event eventually outgrew the log cabin. In 2002, the Country Cabin II was built nearby to accommodate larger audiences. The venue, which features a large stage, hosts local musicians and bands performing bluegrass, country and old-time music every Sunday. In addition, the venue hosts clogging and line-dancing classes. Every September, the Country Cabin also hosts the annual Dock Boggs Festival.

The original cabin, which has also served as a community center, mattress factory and residence, is listed on the National Register of Historic Places, according to the *Roanoke Times*.

BIRTHPLACE OF COUNTRY MUSIC MUSEUM

The city of Bristol, Virginia, is home to a unique and intimate theater inside of the Birthplace of Country Music Museum, which opened in 2014. The museum celebrates the historic 1927 Bristol Sessions, which has been called the "Big Bang" of country music. During the sessions, producer Ralph Peer

Local bluegrass and old-time Appalachian music is often performed inside the theater at the Birthplace of Country Music Museum in Bristol, Virginia. *From the* Bristol Herald Courier.

recorded some of the earliest country music in America and featured the legendary Carter Family and Jimmie Rodgers.

The one-hundred-seat performance theater at the museum is "acoustically perfect" for performances, according to the museum organization. The theater can also host film screenings, presentations, corporate conferences and other events.

Farm and Fun Time, a reimagined classic radio program, is also held regularly at the theater. It is broadcast and streamed live the second Thursday of each month before a studio audience at the museum's theater. In addition, the program is also held quarterly at the nearby Paramount Theatre. The program spotlights the best in roots music touring artists.

In addition to the theater, the Birthplace of Country Music Museum also features various exhibits about the region's rich musical heritage and special exhibits.

OLDE WEST DINNER AND WALLACE THEATERS

The Olde West Dinner Theatre operated for about two decades near the Tri-Cities Airport in Sullivan County, Tennessee. It was a popular establishment where actors and actresses performed every night while guests enjoyed the show and a meal.

Kingsport businessman Fred "Pal" Barger opened the dinner theater in 1966. Barger had previously, in 1956, opened his first Pal's Sudden Service on Revere Street in Kingsport. Additional Pal's locations opened across the region, including Elizabethton and Johnson City.

The dinner theater's first performance was a production of *The Rainmaker*.

Barger helped the theater with selecting the cast and shows from New York City, according to an East Tennessee State University Alumni Association article.

When Barger's father died in 1971, he gained control of his father's Skoby's restaurant. After a few years of hamburgers and hot dogs at Pals and fine dining at Skoby's, Barger decided to sell the Olde West Dinner Theatre and expanded the hot dog business, according to the alumni article.

The Olde West staged several situational comedies, a major musical and a dramatic selection during its season. It also occasionally booked a road show.

"The entertainment value comes first at the Olde West," Director Rick Cannon told the *Kingsport Times-News*. "Everything is geared for an evening of fun."

The theater appears to have closed in 1987, according to newspaper reports. In 1998, the Olde West Dinner Theatre transitioned into the Highlander Dinner Theatre.

The Boone Dam chapter of the Veterans of Foreign Wars acquired the property a short time after the last show. The veterans group stayed there for a couple years before the Olde West Dinner Theatre reopened in 1991.

"The Olde West has returned!" the *Bristol Herald Courier* exclaimed. "For many years, the dinner theater near Tri-Cities Regional Airport in Blountville provided great entertainment for an evening out. The plays were interesting because the audience had such close advantage to the stage."

The newspaper reported that J.C. Mullins of Kingsport had restored the theater building with new carpet, curtains and western décor. The venue closed in early 1998 and transitioned into the Scottish-themed Highlander Dinner Theatre, which was co-owned by Charles "Dee" Bailey, according to the *Bristol Herald Courier*.

The Highlander relocated in late 2000 to the 200 block of East Main Street in Johnson City. In 2020, Chris Maloney, a South Carolina native, opened the Wallace Theatre at the Main Street site. Maloney had relocated to Johnson City, where he reignited a passion for improvisation, live theater and film. The Wallace name was acquired from a previous longtime business known as Wallace Shoes, which dissolved as a company in the 1990s.

INTERNATIONAL STORYTELLING CENTER

Located in the heart of historic downtown Jonesborough, Tennessee, the Mary B. Martin Storytelling Center opened in June 2002 and is dedicated to the international storytelling movement.

The $10 million facility, a part of the International Storytelling Center, features a ninety-five-seat theater, where storytellers weave stories for audiences.

The venue's history began in 1973, when the first National Storytelling Festival was held in Jonesborough, the state's oldest town. At the time, a hay wagon carrying about six storytellers parked near the courthouse and attracted dozens of people, according to festival organizer Jimmy Neil Smith.

"It was the first event devoted exclusively to the art of storytelling in the world," said Smith, according to the Associated Press. "It ignited a storytelling movement, a storytelling renaissance."

The annual festival has grown to attract thousands of visitors, which ultimately led to the creation of the center on Main Street. The site also includes a three-acre park with multiple storytelling sites. The theater is an intimate space where storytellers in residence perform from May to October.

MORE THEATER VENUES

Other unique specialty theater venues in the region include the Boone's Creek Opry, where local bluegrass and other genres are showcased each Saturday in rural Washington County, Tennessee; the 1940s-era Kingsport Civic Auditorium; and the Niswonger Performing Arts Center, a modern show house adjacent to Greeneville High School.

In addition, theater performances have been held at Viking Hall, an arena with a stage at Tennessee High School in Bristol, and Freedom Hall, a similar venue in Johnson City adjacent to Science Hill High School. Other area high schools also feature theaters, including a new modern venue at West Ridge High School in Blountville. High schools in Abingdon, Virginia; Elizabethton, Tennessee; and Washington County, Tennessee, all feature theaters and auditoriums with stages.

10

OUTDOOR DRAMAS

Outdoor dramas have been so popular in the Tri-Cities region that the State of Tennessee and the Commonwealth of Virginia have named local dramas their official state dramas.

The country's first outdoor drama was held on July 5, 1937, on Roanoke Island at Manteo, North Carolina, according to a 1983 article published by the North Carolina Center for Public Policy Research.

Paul Green, a Pulitzer Prize–winning playwright from Chapel Hill, called his new play *The Lost Colony* a "symphonic drama." Green blended music, dance and drama into a new American genre. That play celebrated the 350th birthday of Virginia Dare, the first European child born in America. The drama was held at a Manteo amphitheater, where thousands of people could enjoy the show.

DRAMA AT SYCAMORE SHOALS

In 2024, *Liberty! The Saga of Sycamore Shoals*, the official outdoor drama of the State of Tennessee, celebrated its forty-fifth season at Sycamore Shoals State Historic Park in Elizabethton. It is held every summer in the Fort Watauga Amphitheater, a unique venue near the banks of the Watauga River.

Featuring a cast of local performers who portray pioneer settlers and Native Americans, *Liberty!* depicts the significant history of Sycamore Shoals during the late eighteenth century.

An outdoor drama known as *Liberty!* is performed every summer at Sycamore Shoals State Historic Park in Elizabethton. *From the* Elizabethton Star.

The concept of outdoor drama offers a unique theatrical performance format, one that includes theatrical lighting, professional sound and a host of unexpected effects. *Liberty!* completely immerses its audiences in life in early Tennessee history.

Sycamore Shoals State Historic Park was established in 1975 and features numerous attractions, including a museum and gift shop, trails, picnic pavilions, a reconstruction of the eighteenth-century Fort Watauga, and a 450-seat amphitheater.

The drama was first named The *Wataugans* and was organized by the Watauga Historical Association. It eventually transitioned into *Liberty!* and is produced by the Friends of Sycamore Shoals State Historic Park.

The *Johnson City Press* featured an article on the history of *The Wataugans* and *Liberty!* in 2007. The drama highlights the strong relationship between the settlers at Fort Watauga and the Cherokee Nation, the Transylvania Purchase that marked the beginning of westward expansion and the formation of the first free and independent government on the American continent.

The Tennessee General Assembly approved a proclamation in 2009 to name the play the state's official outdoor drama.

The outdoor drama *Liberty!* is performed annually at the amphitheater at Fort Watauga at Sycamore Shoals State Historic Park. *From the* Elizabethton Star.

THE TRAIL OF THE LONESOME PINE

John Fox Jr., one of Virginia's best-selling authors, published *The Trail of the Lonesome Pine* in 1908. It eventually sold two million copies. Fox, who died in 1919, resided in Big Stone Gap and wrote several historical romances and period dramas set in the region.

In 1912, *The Trail of the Lonesome Pine* was adapted for the stage and was produced at the New Amsterdam Theater in New York City. By 1916, it had been transformed into a film. Finally, in 1964, *The Trail of the Lonesome Pine* was adapted into a stage play by Earl Hobson Smith and Clara Lou Kelly and was first performed in Big Stone Gap, according to a written history on the outdoor drama.

The Trail of the Lonesome Pine describes the remarkable boom that followed the discovery of coal ore in the mountains surrounding Big Stone Gap and subsequent bust when the ambitious plans for development failed to materialize, according to a National Register of Historic Places nomination form on the June Tolliver House. The storyline follows the romance of Jack Hale, an educated engineer searching for coal, and June Tolliver, an intelligent but unlettered mountain girl and the effect on their lives of her education and his remaining to work in Big Stone Gap.

June Morris, the protype of June Tolliver, boarded at the modified Queen Anne–style home when she went to school in Big Stone Gap. The house has become a historic landmark in the community and is open to the public.

The outdoor drama is performed seasonally in a playhouse next to the June Tolliver House. The playhouse was the vision of Barbara Creasy Polly, who originated the role of Tolliver in 1964 when it was first produced by the Big Stone Gap Music Club. The organization and the Lonesome Pine

The June Tolliver House is located in Big Stone Gap adjacent to the site of the *Trail of the Lonesome Pine* outdoor drama. *Author photo.*

Community Chorale went on to stage the drama during the summer months, according to the drama's written history.

Polly, who also helped with the acquisition of the John Fox House and Museum, died in 2016.

After years of performances, the drama has seen many revisions with new casts and crews. There have been new directors, script changes and music changes, the history states.

In 1994, *The Trail of the Lonesome Pine* was named the official outdoor drama of Virginia. It is one of the longest-running outdoor dramas in the country.

THE STORY OF DAVID CROCKETT

David "Davy" Crocket was an early East Tennessee pioneer, American folk hero, soldier and politician born in Greeneville who died while fighting at the Battle of the Alamo. His story has been interpreted in books, movies and at least one outdoor drama.

Crockett never lived in Rogersville, but his family did. Crockett's grandparents were massacred by Native Americans, and they are buried at Rogers Cemetery just off of Main Street near Crocket Creek. From 1967 to 1971, a group of residents presented the *Davy Crockett Outdoor Drama* and later *The Lion of the West*, which portrayed the life and times of Crockett. It was performed annually each summer.

Mary Clay Lewis, Louise Rogers and Marian Slaughter are said to have been responsible for getting the Crockett-based drama on the stage in the summer of 1967, according to the *Rogersville Review*. The three organized a fundraiser and gathered money to build a stage near the site along North Hasson Street in Rogersville. In addition, the group had to build and paint the set, obtain a script and assemble a cast.

In 1969, *Tennessee Magazine*, a publication of the Holston Electric Co-op, featured the Crockett drama: "On one of the nation's largest outdoor stages with East Tennessee hills as a backdrop, the citizens of Rogersville will again depict the story of one of America's most gallant heroes."

The construction of a new U.S. Highway 11W bypass around Rogersville, the state's second-oldest town, prompted the women to create the drama, the magazine said. In an effort to attract tourists into town, the idea was met with enthusiasm and determination to succeed by the town's citizens, the magazine added.

The outdoor drama eventually ceased production after organizers realized traffic through the downtown area had decreased and it became difficult to get tourists to stop for a show, the *Rogersville Review* later learned from previous performers.

THE MELUNGEON STORY

For less than a decade, organizers and patrons gathered in the small rural community of Sneedville, Tennessee, for the play *Walk Toward the Sunset*. The outdoor drama, written by Kermit Hunter, highlighted the Melungeons' role during the American's Revolutionary War, the settlement of Tennessee and the post–Civil War era.

The drama was launched in 1969, but was canceled in 1972, according to a book by Wayne Winkler, who delved into how leaders in the Sneedville area took the story of mixed-raced residents onto the stage, the *Knoxville News-Sentinel* said.

Throughout the twentieth century, Hancock County was an isolated enclave in the heart of the Appalachian Mountains and about an hour from the nearest city. It was one of the poorest counties in the country and has been home to the Melungeons, dark-skinned mixed-race people.

Two professors from East Tennessee State University suggested the community stage an outdoor drama about the Melungeons in order to bring in visitors. As a result, the community and Hunter, the playwright, developed a play.

Hunter, a prolific playwright born in West Virginia, also wrote *Chucky Jack*, an outdoor drama performed in Gatlinburg, Tennessee; *Horn in the West*, a drama produced in Boone, North Carolina; and *Unto These Hills*, a drama in Cherokee, North Carolina.

THE TIDE OF FREEDOM

As the automobile became more popular in the mid-twentieth century, Americans began to travel, and communities began to develop outdoor dramas to attract visitors. In 1952, *The Tide of Freedom* historic drama in Bristol, Virginia, became the latest addition to the rapidly growing list of outdoor dramas being staged for the entertainment of nomadic American tourists.

Produced by Virginia Intermont College and staged in the school's natural amphitheater, the play was first held in July and August 1952. Newspapers said the "thrilling history of the Appalachian area is dramatically told by C. Ernest Cook, Virginia Intermont English department head."

The Tide of Freedom play was held for only two years, according to the Institute of Outdoor Theatre, a North Carolina–based program that documents America's outdoor dramas.

The story was composed of stories of pioneer history, woven together by the theme of freedom. Colonists, who were confronted with an array of problems along the Atlantic Seaboard, headed to Southwest Virginia and Northeast Tennessee.

Newspaper articles said one of the most stirring scenes in the drama was the Battle of King's Mountain in North Carolina. The British, under General Patrick Ferguson, were defeated by a band of fighters largely recruited from the Bristol area, even though they were outnumbered by the British. The victory was an important one for the colonists.

It was believed that many of those travelers would stop in Bristol to see Daniel Boone, John Sevier, Evan Shelby and other pioneers brought to life on the stage of an outdoor theater.

11

COMMUNITY THEATER

*C*ommunity theaters involve more participants, present more performances and play to more people than any other performing art in the United States, according to the American Association of Community Theatre.

In 2024, there were more than six thousand community theaters in the country, each producing four to six, or more, productions each year. The AACT says the number of performances by community theaters would far exceed the number of professional theater, dance and concert organizations.

The Tri-Cities region has been home to several community theater groups, including Tennessee's oldest. The history of community theater in Johnson City appears to have begun in 1886 at Jobe's Opera House, according to an article on the Johnson City Community Theatre, the oldest such organization in Tennessee and the sixth oldest in the United States.

An 1886 performance of *Queen Ester* was the first community effort in Johnson City to present such entertainment outside of churches and schools, the article states. A group of local residents who enjoyed gathering and reading dramatic literature produced the performance.

The Johnson City Community Theatre has operated under a series of names. From 1904 to 1910, the organization was known as the Johnson City Dramatics Club and performed at the Mountain Branch of the National Home for Disabled Volunteer Soldiers theater, according to the article. It was reorganized in 1924 and renamed the Johnson City Theatre Guild. Later, it became the Little Players of Johnson City in 1946, which was one of several "little theater" groups in the region.

The cast of the play *Romanoff and Juliet* is pictured on the Johnson City Community Theatre stage. *Johnson City Community Theatre.*

During the twentieth century, the organization's playhouses included churches, schools, the Johnson City Country Club, the Veterans Administration center and the Johnson City Auditorium, a theater venue that later became the site of the *Johnson City Press*. In addition, the organization teamed up with the East Tennessee State University Patchwork Players for a presentation of William Shakespeare's *Taming of the Shrew*, which was presented at the university's amphitheater.

The organization moved into a building on Maple Street in 1959, where it remained into the twenty-first century. Members believed the connotation of "little" was inappropriate, so they changed the name to the Johnson City Community Theatre.

Converted from an old church, the Maple Street site functioned as a theater-in-the-round before moving to a more proscenium-style venue.

The first production at the site was *The Curious Savage*, a play directed by Daryl Frank, the wife of Harold "Bud" Frank, from East Tennessee State University. The Franks were heavily involved in the Johnson City Community Theater.

In the 1980s, the Johnson City Community Theater began to evolve and produce more adult-themed shows and musicals, according to the *Johnson City Press*.

Since 1912, the theater company has been continuously producing yearlong seasons of productions, which have included plays from George Bernard Shaw and Tennessee Williams to modern classic musicals like *Rent* and *All Shook Up*, according to a *Johnson City Press* article in 2017.

THE GUILD

In September 1947, a large, enthusiastic audience enjoyed a theatrical performance of the English comedy *Yes and No* in Kingsport. It was the first production of the Kingsport Theatre Guild, which had formed that year.

The Kingsport Theatre Guild was first established in 1947 and has performed at various venues around the city. *City of Kingsport Archives.*

The Kingsport Theatre Guild presents a variety of stage productions each year with comedy, drama, music and mystery. Since its inception, the organization has performed at a variety of venues, including a barn on Eden's Ridge, school auditoriums, church fellowship halls, a community center on Sullivan Street, the Fine Arts Center on historic Church Circle and the Renaissance Center.

In 1986, for the fortieth season opener, the guild performed *Something to Hide*. At that point, the guild had been described as a starting point for individuals who later headed to the bright lights of New York City, some starring in commercials or dancing on Broadway, according to the *Kingsport Times-News*.

In 1992, the guild expanded its board of directors to include more community representatives, and it hired its first staff person in 1993.

The Renaissance Center, which features a 350-seat theater and other facilities, is located in the former John Sevier School. It was renovated in 1991 and has long served as a venue for the Kingsport Theatre Guild. Theatrical performances and concerts are held at the theater throughout the year.

THEATRE BRISTOL

Theatre Bristol, a community theater company, was founded in the 1960s. It launched as the Bristol Children's Theatre. In 1966, the group first performed *Hansel and Gretel* at the former Sullins College Little Theatre, according to the *Bristol Herald Courier*. The college was the perfect site for children's plays and adult productions.

The group was founded by Catherine Fleenor DeCaterina, who grew up in Bristol and studied classical voice and opera at the Juilliard School in New York City, according to an article published in 20017 by *A! Magazine for the Arts*. DeCaterina began after-school drama classes while working at the Episcopal Day School, which led to the creation of Theatre Bristol.

The children's theater was incorporated in the 1970s and began to rehearse and perform at various locations before finally relocating to downtown Bristol in the 500 block of State Street. It established a reputation as the only theater of its kind between Roanoke, Virginia, and Nashville, Tennessee.

In 1977, the children's theater created the Bristol Theatre Academy, which provided drama education for adults and children.

Theatre Bristol, a community theater organization, is headquartered adjacent to the historic Paramount Theatre in downtown Bristol. *Author photo.*

Later, in 1978, the name officially changed to Theatre Bristol. A few years later, DeCaterina became instrumental in the rehabilitation of the Paramount, a neglected Bristol landmark near Theatre Bristol. A newspaper article said Harry Daniel, a native Bristolian who was living in California, gave the Paramount to Theatre Bristol, but the group did not plan to move into the old movie house. Instead, the organization formed a separate theater foundation.

"Because of the massive undertaking which the Paramount Theatre will require and because Theatre Bristol occupies and has use of outstanding facilities in United Coal Company's Humanities Center, the board of directors has formed a Paramount Foundation to administer the theater," said Bob Rauchle, Theatre Bristol board chairman.

Theatre Bristol is led by an all-volunteer organization and continued to produce performances in 2024. The organization provides theater camps in the summer as well as workshops and classes, according to its website.

In 1964, a group of local residents established the Dogwood Players of Bristol. It met regularly at local churches and produced plays at an auditorium at Virginia Intermont College.

The Dogwood Players concentrated on sophisticated comedy, according to the *Bristol Herald Courier*. In December 1964, the Players performed their first play, *Candida*, which was directed by Richard Olsen, director of drama at Sullins College.

BLUFF CITY

Eventually, in December 1980, the Dogwood Players combined with the Bluff City Community Theatre to form the Dogwood Community Theatre. The newly formed group performed at the Slater Center, a venue owned by the city of Bristol, Tennessee. The Dogwood Community Theatre continued to produce plays through the 1980s.

The Bluff City Community Theatre, which the Dogwood Players partnered with, was originally created in 1976 in the small town of Bluff City, Tennessee. The group produced a performance of *Arsenic and Old Lace* at the Bluff City Rescue Hall. The next year, the new community theater performed *The Music Man* in the fellowship hall at Bluff City Methodist Church. Then, in 1978, they returned to the Rescue Hall, according to articles in the *Bristol Herald Courier*.

Community theaters have long entertained the residents of Greeneville. One of those organizations, the Little Theatre, first appeared in 1963 with a performance of *You Can't Take It with You*. The play was presented at the Roby School Auditorium and debuted one week after President John F. Kennedy was assassinated in Dallas, Texas.

GREENEVILLE THEATER

"Weeks of planning and rehearsals, plus getting the old Roby Auditorium in working condition, collided head-on with a national tragedy," said Dan Spice, co-president of the Greeneville Greene County History Museum, according to the *Greeneville Sun*. "The cast and director Betty Haberstick decided that people might need a diversion for a few hours after all the bad news of the day."

"The show must go on," Haberstick and her husband told an attentive audience that night. The couple appeared on the stage in front of the curtain and explained why they were continuing the performance despite the recent tragedy.

The Roby Auditorium later became known as the Haberstick Auditorium and long served as a Little Theatre venue. In 1995, the Little Theatre acquired the historic Capitol Theatre on Main Street and launched a major renovation. The theater reopened in 2002, but the expensive renovations ultimately led to its demise due to mounting debts. The federal government foreclosed on the Capitol property in 2008, and the Little Theatre folded, according to newspaper articles.

A few years later, a group of actors and actresses created the Greeneville Theatre Guild. Officially organized in 2014, the new organization held its first performance season in 2015. Performances were held at the Capitol Theatre, which was purchased by businessman Tracy Solomon in 2014.

The Greeneville Theatre Guild acquired its own building on West Depot Street in downtown Greeneville in 2015. The organization then began to restore the building, which has served as a grocery store, a law firm and a tobacco warehouse, according to WJHL-TV.

The COVID-19 pandemic delayed work on the new venue, but it is expected to open in 2025. The Theater on Depot will have a black box venue and plenty of space for shows and performers, according to the WJHL article.

FANTASTIC THEATERS

The Road Company served as a professional community theater in the twentieth century. It was founded in Johnson City by Bob Leonard. At that time, the company had no home stage and toured its shows throughout the region.

"Traditionally we create our material through improvisation," Leonard told the *Kingsport Times-News*. "Two shows, 'Chatauqua' and 'Horsepower,' were the products of collaboration with the writer. The Road Company attempts to use its theater craft to reflect the community in which we live. We create plays which come out of this area."

The 1970s brought Fantastick Productions, a touring theater company, to the Tri-Cities. The organization, which was based in Fall Branch, Tennessee, toured children's plays throughout the region with as much scenery and equipment that could fit in one vehicle, the *Kingsport Times-News* said.

The goal of Fantastick Productions was to bring shows "performed by adults, for children, to places where live theater is not ordinarily seen," according to the *Times-News* article.

Schools and other auditoriums served as venues for the company, which held four productions a year, including two for children and two for adults.

Kimball Sterling, an East Tennessee State University theater graduate, and his wife managed the company.

In 1971, it was described as the only theatrical touring company in East Tennessee. The company consisted of nine professional actors and a company staff. Fantastick Productions was no longer operating in the early 1980s, and Sterling became a prominent local auctioneer.

The small town of Erwin has hosted a few theater groups over the years, including the Erwin Community Players. Organized in 1949, the Players produced a performance of *Your Uncle Dudley* during its first year at the Municipal Hall Auditorium in downtown Erwin. They met regularly at the YMCA Club Room in Erwin.

Built in the 1920s, Municipal Hall was located on Gay Street near the Unicoi County Courthouse. The first floor was used by the town for storage, including an old fire engine, and classroom space. The second and third floors were occupied by the historic theater, which was used for decades by the community, and the fourth floor was used by the local Masonic Lodge.

The old building was destroyed by fire in 2009. It was demolished and turned into a parking lot.

OLD TOWN THEATER

The Jonesborough Repertory Theatre is one of the Tri-Cities region's most prominent theater companies. Its history dates to about 1970, when a group of volunteers began working together to take part in Tennessee's Statehood Days celebration. Jimmy Neil Smith, a former Jonesborough mayor, wrote a play that was performed at the celebration in Nashville's Centennial Park, according to a written history of the theater company.

The Jonesborough Repertory Theatre was soon formed and then chartered on January 24, 1971. A repertory theater is a company in which each member takes an active part in the matters of the theater, including business and production. The new group presented *Generation* one month later.

For the next few years, the *Bristol Herald Courier* said the organization presented performances wherever stages were available, including the theater at the Mountain Home veterans' site, David Crockett High School and the Washington County Courthouse in Jonesborough, where a courtroom drama was presented during Fourth of July celebrations in 1971.

In 1973, Dr. Opie Haws, a local physician, leased the group a warehouse adjacent to his office building on Main Street. Renovations were completed with the help of volunteers. New platforms, partitions and doors, as well as a control booth and dimmer board, were installed, the *Bristol Herald Courier* reported.

The theater company eventually purchased the property in the 1980s and conducted a complete renovation. Just to name a few things, the group rearranged the theater's seats, put up stage lights, added a privacy fence and installed new siding in 1988 and 1989.

Additional improvements were completed in 2000. Then, in 2003, the Jonesborough Repertory Theatre began a partnership with the town. It led to growth of the theater company, further building improvements, a costume shop, education courses and relationships with other local theaters, according to the organization's written history.

The JRT hosts eight main stage productions a season, as well as travel shows, educational classes for school children and theater outreach for senior citizens.

Mountain City

Community theater efforts led to the establishment of Heritage Hall in rural Mountain City, Tennessee. A small group of volunteers raised money, organized labor and oversaw renovations of the town's former high school auditorium. The venue, which seats 388 people, opened in September 2005 and provides live entertainment for the community, including theater and concerts.

Up until 2005, Mountain City did not have a performance stage. Theatrical events were held at local churches, fellowship halls, community centers and school gymnasiums. The old high school, which had an auditorium for theatrical performances, originally closed in 1966. Its replacement had no auditorium, according to information from Heritage Hall.

The Johnson County Community Theater was established in the mid-1980s by Bill and Kathy Terrill, Bob Morrison and Jim Gilley. The group performed at the high school, as well as Ralph Stout Park in Mountain City. In 1988, the organization presented a show at Washington College Academy.

12

COLLEGE THEATERS

When military veteran and actor Harold "Bud" Frank arrived to teach at East Tennessee State University in 1953, there was no theater program.

He said, "I like the area very much," even though the school had no theater program to speak of, according to a *Johnson City Press* article about Frank's retirement in 1985. "But that was the challenge," the opportunity to build something from the ground up.

Students who came to ETSU in Johnson City were "fresh, unimbued with a false sense of sophistication. I felt as though this area nurtured a great deal of talent that was undeveloped and needed encouragement," he said.

Frank and his wife, Daryl Frank, spent years developing the university's theater program and helped launch the careers of countless actors and actresses.

"Educational theater is a laboratory," Frank told the newspaper. "I wasn't driven to do plays by their popularity, although building an audience was a concern, and rightly so. There is a value that inherently has to be educated in audiences. You don't get it by presenting 'pap.' You get it by presenting substance."

East Tennessee State University's theater department and various theater groups have presented programs in several venues throughout its history, which began in the early twentieth century. Most department productions have been held at the Bud Frank Theatre in Gilbreath Hall, the university's first building. Sidney Gilbreath was the university's first president.

Karen Brewster, who served as the chair of the department of theater and dance, said the venue had some problems as a functional space.

Top: Harold "Bud" Frank first began teaching at East Tennessee State University in 1953. He is widely recognized as the founder of theater at the institution. *East Tennessee State University.*

Bottom: The Bud Frank Theater at East Tennessee State University is used for cinematic shows, particularly those not available elsewhere. *East Tennessee State University.*

In 2020, the university opened the Martin Center for the Arts, a $53 million facility that includes performance and instructional spaces for students, faculty and community.

Inside, patrons, students and artists will find three performance venues, including the 1,200-seat ETSU Foundation Grand Hall, the 200-plus-seat Powell Recital Hall and a black box theater known as the Bert C. Bach Theatre. The black box theater allows the venue to change the staging and seating in any way performances demand, according to Brewster. The facility, which features a box office, faces State of Franklin Road and the main ETSU campus.

In 2023, the Bud Frank Theatre reopened after undergoing significant renovations along with the redesign of Gilbreath Hall, which is located in the center of the ETSU campus. The theater transformed into the only art cinema in the region outside of Asheville, North Carolina, according to the university.

"This is important, because half of the films released, indeed, half the Oscar contenders, do not play in Northeast Tennessee on initial release," said Dr. Matthew Holtmeier, an associate professor in the Department of Literature and Language.

The new theater reopened with a performance by musicians in ETSU's Bluegrass, Old-Time and Roots Music Studies and a screening of the silent film *Our Hospitality*. The theater later showcased *Annihilation*, *Rocky Horror Picture Show*, *Frankenstein* and *White Christmas*.

Various performances, lectures and other community gatherings have also been held at the Martha Street Culp Auditorium in the D.P. Culp University Center at ETSU.

DERTHICK HALL

Derthick Hall, one of the first buildings constructed on the Milligan University campus, featured a designated area for chapel and a theater. It served the college for decades as a performance hall for various theater groups and classes.

In 1978, Milligan completely renovated the Derthick Hall theater, which was named after the college's eighth president, Henry Derthick. Derthick arrived at Milligan in 1917 and served as president until 1940.

"We think one of the most beneficial results of the renovation project will be the auditorium, or little theatre," former Milligan president Jess Johnson told the *Elizabethton Star*.

Milligan University near Johnson City has been home to several theater venues over the years, including the auditorium at the former Derthick Hall. *Milligan University.*

Johnson said the auditorium was designed to accommodate slightly more than 250 people for drama, films and concerts. "The stage has been expanded by four feet, a lighting system added, and new seating is being installed," Johnson said.

The Derthick auditorium gave Milligan three settings for plays, which also included Seeger Hall, where major productions were held, and Sutton Hall, a setting for dinner theater productions.

According to Milligan history, Derthick Hall was constructed on the site of the college's first building, which was constructed in 1867 for the Buffalo Male and Female Institute.

Following the massive 1978 renovation, Derthick Hall was renovated twice more.

Seeger Chapel, which was built in 1967, features two auditoriums that will accommodate 1,300. When built, it was the largest structure of its kind in East Tennessee with thirty-one thousand square feet of floor space, according to the *Johnson City Press*.

The chapel, a popular venue for theater and music productions, is 177 feet long and 76 feet wide, and at the roof ridge it is 57 feet above the ground level. At the top of the giant spire, it is 169 feet above the ground level, the newspaper reported.

Seeger was also constructed with a forty-by-twenty-six-foot stage, large enough to accommodate a one-hundred-piece symphony orchestra. The Seeger facility was not designed for drama productions, officials said.

In 2008, Milligan officially opened the Elizabeth Leitner Gregory Center for the Liberal Arts, which replaced the old auditorium at Derthick Hall. The Gregoy Center is home the McGlothlin-Street Theatre, a three-hundred-seat auditorium. The new building houses the college's theater department and its humanities program.

KEYSER AND ADAY

Virginia Highlands Community College, which was established in 1967 to serve the residents of Washington County, Smyth County and the city of Bristol, Virginia, did not at first have a theater program. Early on, its administrators wanted to create a theater program that could partner with Abingdon's Barter Theatre. The Barter's Robert Porterfield agreed to work with the program if they found the right person to lead it.

The *Bristol Herald Courier* reported that Van Keyser, a graduate of nearby Emory & Henry College, was leading a theater program at another Virginia community college. He was recruited to start a new VHCC program and officially joined the faculty in 1970.

Two years later, Keyser recruited Gary Aday, whom he met at Northwestern University, to further develop the program. Since then, the pair have overseen more than one hundred productions at VHCC.

When the Learning Resource Center at VHCC was built in 1986, it included a new theater auditorium. The first play performed on the new stage was Tennessee Williams's *Suddenly Last Summer*. It was renamed the Keyser-Aday Theatre at VHCC in 2009.

NORTHEAST

Northeast State Community College in Blountville, Tennessee, unveiled its regional performing arts theater in 2008. "This will be one of the finest performing arts centers in our region," former Northeast State president Dr. Bill Locke said in 2008. "The biggest thing the theater will do is provide a place where people from across the region can come and participate in cultural events, in a beautiful setting that is close to the center of the Tri-Cities."

The thirty-six-thousand-square foot building contains a five-hundred-seat theater, fine arts classrooms and a physical education laboratory, according to a news release issued in 2008. The theater almost tripled the performance space that was available at Northeast State's two-hundred-seat auditorium.

Northeast State was first established as a technical school in 1966. It eventually became Northeast State Community College in 1990.

Theater has been celebrated at King University in Bristol, Tennessee, for more than a century. Various productions have been held in at least two locations on campus.

The Women's Auxiliary Building was originally constructed in 1918 to house the university's dining services. It has been more recently referred to as the Fine Arts Building. It houses a small theater, an art workshop, a dance studio and a gallery.

Another King building, Memorial Chapel, seats approximately 350 people. It features a large auditorium with a stage and has been used for various functions since it was built in 1932, including chapel services, convocations and theater productions. The building also includes classrooms and offices.

King's theater programs and various student organizations have also partnered with area theater groups, including other colleges.

CLINCH VALLEY

A full-fledged theater has been operating at the University of Virginia's College at Wise, and its predecessor, Clinch Valley College, since the 1970s. Clinch Valley College, which is in the small town of Wise, began enrolling students in September 1954. It became a four-year college in 1968 and continued to grow over the next few years.

In 1973, the college began to build a modern theater workshop complex. It opened the following year and included a 150-seat auditorium. Prior to the theater's opening, drama performances were held in the school's gymnasium, according to newspaper articles.

"Whenever we did a show out here, that was the cultural event of the season," the school's drama professor, Dr. Charles Lewis, told the *Roanoke Times*.

With the new theater's opening, the college began offering courses in directing, scene design, stage carpentry, make-up, costuming, playwrighting, criticism, theater history and acting.

In 1998, Clinch Valley College was renamed the University of Virginia's College at Wise.

A new $14.4 million fine arts and performing arts facility known as the Gilliam Center for the Arts opened on campus in 2009. The name was chosen to honor the Gilliam family, which has a history of advocacy for education and cultural activities throughout the region, the college said in a written statement.

The center includes a full-scale theater that features scenic and costume studios, a rehearsal studio and a courtyard suitable for performances.

TUSCULUM

Prior to a theater being constructed at Tusculum University in 1965, drama and music productions were held at various venues in Greeneville, Tennessee. The Annie Hogan Byrd Fine Arts Center and Chapel officially opened in 1965. It is home to the Marilyn duBrisk Theatre, a 692-seat auditorium with "excellent acoustics," according to the university. It now houses the university's Arts Outreach Program. In addition, the center is home to the Behan Arena Theatre, a two-hundred-plus-seat black box theater.

Marilyn duBrisk came to Greene County in 1984 and became the artist-in-residence for the Greeneville school system. Later, in 1991, she accepted the same position at Tusculum, where she retired from in 2020. During her tenure, duBrisk directed numerous performances at the Annie Hogan Byrd. The venue was dedicated to duBrisk in 2021.

Established in 1794, Tusculum College is the oldest college in Tennessee. By the 1900s, dramatic and musical performances were being held at Tusculum's gymnasium, as well as several local churches. One group, the Pioneer Players, performed at various venues through the 1960s.

EMORY AND HENRY

In 1949, a fine arts professor at Emory & Henry College said he was trying to stimulate interest in dramatics and theater in college and at area high schools.

"The effort at Emory & Henry is not to develop a dramatics department as such, but to stimulate an interest in theater and to get the students who are going to be teachers, ministers, and church workers and give them some knowledge of drama and the literature of the drama," said Dr. Marius Blesi.

The professor said he believed there was an "alarming disinterestedness in the high schools," because students came from areas where "people have never seen good plays." Emory & Henry hosted a regional high school drama festival in 1949.

Dramatic and musical performances have been held at Emory & Henry near Meadowview, Virginia, at various venues, including a gymnasium, the auditorium at the E.E. Wiley Hall and the Black Box Theatre. Wiley Hall, which was built in 1928, replaced a nearly identical structure at the site. The previous building featured an auditorium with a balcony. The Black Box Theatre has transitioned into a career and professional development center.

In 2015, Emory & Henry officially opened the Woodrow W. McGlothlin Center for the Arts, a $28.5 million facility dedicated to theater, music and the arts. The center, which sits between Wiley Hall and Carriger Hall on the college's historic campus, features the 461-seat Main Stage Theatre and a new 120-seat black box theater. It also features a curated art gallery, dressing rooms, production areas, theater department offices and a radio station studio.

Former Programs

Several former colleges in the Tri-Cities region have also hosted theatrical performances, including Virginia Intermont College, Sullins College, Stonewall Jackson College, Martha Washington College and Villa Marie Academy.

Virginia Intermont College, which operated from 1884 to 2017 and is now vacant, was home to the Worrell Fine Arts Center. The center was constructed in 1961 and featured a theater and a recital hall. The college's art, music and theater programs were also housed in the building.

Formerly known as Virginia Intermont's Little Theatre, the theater facility was renamed after Dorothy Cigrand Trayer, a 1931 graduate of the college. The campus also features an auditorium theater inside the Harrison-Jones Memorial Hall, which was completed in 1967 and could seat 982 people.

Sullins College, a former institution in Bristol, was first established around the time of the Civil War in the 1800s. It was originally located near downtown Bristol until its building burned in 1915, and reopened on Glenway Avenue, where it operated through the 1970s.

The campus had a few venues for theater performances. In 1945, the college began an expansion project, which included the construction of the Baskerville Liberty and Virginia Hall. The Baskerville building featured the Little Theatre, where movies and performances were held, and Virginia was home to the Sylvan Theatre.

Sullins had a handful of theater programs, including the Sullins Repertory Theatre for Children.

BIBLIOGRAPHY

American Association of Community Theatre. "Community Theatre's Impact." https://aact.org.

Big Stone Gap (VA) Post. Various articles on theaters.

Bristol Herald Courier (Bristol, TN and VA). Various articles on theaters. Including predecessor newspapers, 1908–2023.

Capitol Theatre. "About Us." www.capitolgreeneville.org.

Cinema Treasures. Various entries. https://cinematreasures.org.

The *Comet*. Various articles on theaters. Johnson City, TN. 1884–1913.

Dawidziak, Mark. *The Barter Theatre Story: Love Made Visible*. Boone, NC: Appalachian State University Press, 1982.

Early, O.J. "Revitalized Bud Frank Theatre Coming to Life." East Tennessee State University, https://www.etsu.edu.

Elizabethton (TN) Star. Various articles on theaters. Including predecessor newspapers, 1900–2023.

Erwin (TN) Record. Various articles on theaters. Including predecessor newspapers, 1926–2024.

Friends of Sycamore Shoals State Historic Park. "Liberty! The Saga of Sycamore Shoals." https://www.friendsofsycamoreshoals.org.

Grace, Leslie. "Theatre Bristol Has a Rich History." *Arts Alliance Mountain Empire*, October 2017.

Greeneville (TN) Sun. Various articles on theaters. Including predecessor newspapers.

Herald and Tribune (Jonesborough, TN). Various articles on theaters.

BIBLIOGRAPHY

Heritage Hall Theatre. "Our History." https://heritagehalltheatre.org.

Johnson City Press. Various articles on theaters. Including predecessor newspapers, 1914–2021.

Johnson, Lea. "Owner of the Stateline Drive-In Theatre Wants to Sell the Property." WJHL-TV, 2023.

Jonesborough Repertory Theatre. "About Jonesborough Repertory Theatre." https://www.jonesboroughtheatre.com.

Kingsport (TN) Times-News. Various articles on theaters. Including predecessor newspapers, 1916–1992.

Knoxville (TN) News-Sentinel. Various articles on theaters. Including predecessor newspapers.

Lines, Patrick. "150 Years of Milligan College: Derthick Hall." Milligan Stampede, September 22, 2106. https://www.milliganstampede.com.

Lockwood, Louisa. "Outdoor Drama." *NC Insight*, February 1983.

National WWII Museum. "The Third War Loan." https://www.nww2m.com.

Newspapers.com. Various articles on theaters.

New York Film Academy. "The History of Drive-in Movie Theaters (And Where Are They Now)." https://www.nyfa.edu.

Paramount Bristol. "About Paramount Bristol." https://paramountbristol.org.

Ray, Stahl. *Greater Johnson City: A Pictorial History*. Virginia Beach, VA: Donning Company, 1983.

Rogersville (TN) Review. Various articles on theaters. 1914–2021.

Sorrell, Robert. Images of America: *Roan Mountain*. Charleston, SC: Arcadia Publishing, 2014.

State Theater Kingsport. "About Us." https://www.statetheaterkingsport.com.

Tennessee Historical Commission. "Tennessee Historical Commission Viewer." https://tnmap.tn.gov.

Theatre Historical Society of America. "Quonset Hut Theatres." https://historictheatres.org.

Tomahawk (Mountain City, TN). Various articles on theaters. Including predecessor newspapers. 1945–1966.

Trail of the Lonesome Pine. "History of the Drama." http://www.trailofthelonesomepine.com.

Tusculum University. "Marilyn duBrisk Theatre." https://arts.tusculum.edu.

U.S. Department of the Interior. "Appalachia Commercial Historic District." National Register of Historic Places nomination form.

———. "Barter Theatre." National Register of Historic Places nomination form.

————. "Bristol Commercial Historic District." National Register of Historic Places nomination form.

————. "Carter Family Thematic Nomination." National Register of Historic Places nomination form.

————. "Country Cabin." National Register of Historic Places nomination form.

————. "Johnson City Commercial Historic District." National Register of Historic Places nomination form.

————. "June Tolliver House." National Register of Historic Places nomination form.

————. "Moonlite Theatre." National Register of Historic Places nomination form.

————. "Mountain Branch, National Home for Disabled Volunteer Soldiers." National Register of Historic Places nomination form.

————. "Paramount Theatre." National Register of Historic Places nomination form.

————. "Stonega Historic District." National Register of Historic Places nomination form.

————. "St. Paul Historic District." National Register of Historic Places nomination form.

U.S. Department of Veterans Affairs. "Building 35—The Theater (Memorial Hall)." https://www.va.gov.

INDEX

ABOUT THE AUTHOR

*C*uthor Robert Sorrell is an award-winning journalist, freelance writer and real estate agent. Based in Elizabethton, Tennessee, and a *Bristol Herald Courier* reporter, he has contributed to numerous publications and is the author of regional history books. He has also twice received the Award of Distinction from the East Tennessee Historical Society.